Speaker's Corner Books

is a provocative new series designed to stimulate, educate, and foster discussion on significant public policy topics. Written by experts in a variety of fields, these brief and engaging books should be read by anyone interested in the trends and issues that shape our society.

For more information, visit our Web site,
  www.fulcrumbooks.com

One Nation Under Guns

an Essay on an American Epidemic

One Nation Under Guns
an Essay on an American Epidemic

Arnold Grossman

Fulcrum Publishing
Golden, Colorado

Library of Congress Cataloging-in-Publication Data

Grossman, Arnold.
  One nation under guns : an essay on an American epidemic / by Arnold Grossman.
    p. cm. -- (Speaker's corner books)
  ISBN-13: 978-1-55591-557-5 (pbk.)
  ISBN-10: 1-55591-557-4
  1. Firearms ownership--United States. 2. Firearms--Law and legis-lation--United States. 3. Firearms and crime--United States. 4. Firearms industry and trade--United States. 5. Gun control--United States. I. Title. II. Series.
  HV8059.G78 2006
  363.33--dc22

                              2006014941

Printed in Canada by Friesens Corporation
0 9 8 7 6 5 4 3 2

Editorial: Sam Scinta, Faith Marcovecchio
Cover and interior design: Jack Lenzo

Fulcrum Publishing
16100 Table Mountain Parkway, Suite 300
Golden, Colorado 80403
(800) 992-2908 • (303) 277-1623
www.fulcrumbooks.com

For the eighty-two Americans,
including the eight children, who die
of gun violence every day in America

Contents

Foreword

War on Terror, and We Supply the Weapons

America's war on terror is the first war in our history where we have fully collaborated in our enemy arming himself. Right now, at least three dozen individuals on the federal terrorist watch list have freely bought weapons in gun shops in this country. That is, three dozen that we know of.

If this makes sense to you, you have a keener sense of logic than I have. We have to partly disrobe to get into an airport. Our bank accounts are subject to search by federal officials. Law enforcement agents operating under the Patriot Act can enter our homes and offices without a warrant and search our premises. If our security services consider us a threat, at least in theory we can be indefinitely detained without due process of law. All this and more in the name of the war on terrorism.

But if a terrorist, even one we suspect and are watching, wants to buy any number of high-caliber, high-performance, armor-piercing, assault-capable weapons and virtually any amount of ammunition to go with them, he is free to do so. I don't know about you, but I think something's wrong with this picture.

This situation is simply the triumph of paranoia combined with the hammerlock of political lobbying over good American common sense. We can all have our own views about citizen ownership of firearms, and as a western gun owner, I do. But there is simply no way anyone can justify placing the freedom of terrorists to buy weapons over homeland safety and national security. In an age of terrorism, this is simply insane.

I'd be amazed if one American in a hundred, maybe even one in a thousand, knows that the doors of American gun shops are freely open to terrorists. Because if they did, and if they cared at all for the safety of their families and communities, they'd come howling down on the White House and Congress to "do something," to stop this craziness now.

A few years back, before 9/11 and before anyone knew who he was, Osama bin Laden sent an agent to America to buy armor-piercing .50-caliber rifles. Today that same agent could still buy them. There is no way that situation makes any sense. How in God's name can the argument that an American citizen should be able to buy an armor-piercing sniper rifle be extended to include Osama bin Laden?

A former senior Bureau of Alcohol, Tobacco, Firearms and Explosives (ATF) official has said that we are "the candy store for guns in the world" and that America is "absolutely" the best place for terrorists to buy weapons. By the way, those are terrorists who are out to kill us and who have already killed well over 3,000 Americans.

This total craziness is justified by those who argue that Americans have a constitutional right to own guns. The last time I checked, Osama bin Laden was not an American citizen. We also have a constitutional right to travel. But we still get searched at airports. We have a constitutional right to privacy in our homes. But the FBI can now break in without a warrant. I still don't understand why owning guns is so much a greater right than all our other constitutional rights that it requires us to sacrifice the safety of our families, homes, and communities to protect it.

Shortly after 9/11, President Bush told the United Nations, "We have a responsibility to deny weapons to terrorists and to actively prevent private citizens from providing them." Every action of this administration and its supporters in Congress has been directly opposed to this statement. President Bush signed a law permitting records of gun sales to be destroyed within twenty-four hours. Congress permitted the assault weapons ban to expire. Neither the White House nor Congress will regulate arms sales at gun shows. Legislation is pending to *reduce* the authority of the ATF to track criminal gun sales. It is still easy for terrorists to buy weapons in America to be used to kill Americans.

This is a triumph of selfishness over security. It is the ultimate in human folly. It is un-American. And when the next terrorist attack occurs, unlike after the last one, *someone* must be held accountable.

In this new and important essay, Arnold Grossman restores much-needed sanity to an increasingly irrational social dispute.

—Gary Hart, Former U.S. Senator,
Co-Chair, The U.S. Commission on
National Security/21st Century

Acknowledgments

I wish to thank the many people who helped me with this project, including all the Fulcrum family, and especially Sam Scinta, who created this worthy series, Speaker's Corner Books, and who guided me through the process; founder Bob Baron, who, in addition to knowing publishing, also knows the importance of baseball; and Faith Marcovecchio, a gifted editor whose insight and professionalism gave me a better book.

I am indebted to former Senator Gary Hart for his support and insight and to the dedicated people at the Brady Campaign to Prevent Gun Violence, particularly Brian Malte, the tireless grassroots director who works night and day to make this a safer country; Sarah and Jim Brady, who will never give up the good fight to stop the gun violence epidemic; Denny Hennigan and Mike Barnes, for their continuing commitment to and achievements in behalf of the cause; all the staff in Washington and the regional offices, along with the many members of Million Mom March and Colorado Ceasefire; to Tom Mauser, who continues to carry the banner of safety for our children in tribute to the memory of Daniel, the son he lost at Columbine; to my good friend and fellow co-founder of SAFE Colorado, John Head; to our bipartisan board: former governor Dick Lamm and his wife, Dottie, who did so much to enlist young people in our efforts, the late John Love, also a former Colorado governor, J. D. MacFarlane, Mary Estill Buchanan, friend and mentor Rabbi Steven Foster, David Sprecace, and Wally Stealy.

I also wish to offer special thanks to Sandra Dallas, author and loyal friend, who supported and encouraged me every step of the way.

And finally, I want to thank my wonderful granddaughter, Michaela, who, at age seven, gave me the inspiration to try and do something for the grieving and frightened children of Colorado in the aftermath of Columbine.

Prologue
Another Day, Another Death

A brilliant autumn Saturday. A typical Colorado morning, resplendent with vivid golds and oranges contrasted against a blue that can only exist here. A picture of the hopefulness of another day, at week's end. But then, as quickly as the early newscast fades from the television screen, the morning is clouded, the hope fades with the lead story: The previous night, two friends, eighteen and nineteen, were in a parked car. They were reportedly having an argument. The eighteen-year-old pulled a gun to resolve the argument and shot his friend, who died shortly afterward of a single gunshot to the chest.

Turning off the TV, saddened at the image of a young man's life draining from him as he sat next to his friend holding a murderous weapon, I realize that once again, two young lives are taken, one by the utter finality of death, the other by what could be an irrevocable condemnation to a prison cell for the rest of his life.

I leaf through the newspaper clippings on the desk. There is a story reporting the passage by the

House of Representatives of a bill to grant the nation's gun manufacturers immunity from legal liability for gun deaths caused by products they make and sell. A few weeks earlier, the Senate passed the bill, and now it remains to be signed into law by President George W. Bush, who is quoted as saying he "looks forward to signing the bill," which will make gun manufacturers and dealers the only industry in America that is granted such a shield. The Immunity Bill, essentially a Republican effort, was crafted with the party's most favored lobby, the gun industry, the same industry that helped the GOP take control of the House and the Senate, along with keeping the White House in 2004.

When the president signed the bill (which he did, quickly), he repaid a debt to the NRA, ignoring the implications for the gun epidemic that plagues this nation. It's politics in its basest form. In the world of lobbying and influence peddling, that's life.

Another clipping. This one, a letter to the editor in a local newspaper in which the writer claims it is not merely wrong to hold manufacturers liable for criminal misuse of their products, but that it is an act of cowardice, an attempt to bypass the Constitution and eradicate firearms and destroy the Second Amendment. The writer voices the familiar rallying cry of opponents of gun regulations: that sensible controls are little more than efforts by "the liberal courts" to take away citizens' rights.

What is cowardly about holding the gun industry

accountable for deaths and injury caused by the products it makes and sells? Who is the crowd that appears to rely more and more on liberal activist courts? And why is every attempt at regulation of deadly weapons an anti-gun agenda, even when it is supported by most owners and users of guns?

While supporters of blanket immunity for the gun industry continue to harangue those who call for responsible accountability, the deaths in America continue—nearly 30,000 Americans every year—from the products made by the industry the president and members of Congress want to protect. It was, after all, a gun, a deadly weapon in any hands, and illegal in the hands of an eighteen-year-old, that took the life of an innocent teenager in that car last night.

Today, Saturday, also happens to be a market day all across the national landscape. People flock to farmers' markets for fresh produce, to flea markets for bargains, to antique markets for rare finds.

Some will also flock to another kind of market, not for fresh vegetables, for curios, or for bargains, but for the deadliest of merchandise. It's an American

> **They (guns) are so pervasive in our society because they are so easy to obtain, because politicians, from the president on down, choose to favor the businesses that make and profit from them.**

institution: the gun show, where so many loopholes exist that someone underage, an eighteen-year-old, say, like the boy who shot his friend last night, can illegally buy a handgun—no questions asked. These deadly products will be used to end an argument, to rob a store, to ambush a police officer, to commit suicide or an act of terror. They are so pervasive in our society because they are so easy to obtain, because politicians, from the president on down, choose to favor the businesses that make and profit from them.

Those are sobering thoughts that intrude on a pleasant Saturday morning.

And they need desperately to be addressed.

Chapter 1
A Gun in Every Hand?

In the next five seconds, another handgun will be manufactured somewhere in the United States. In the next two minutes, someone will be shot with a handgun. If today is an average day, eighty-two Americans will die from gunfire by midnight. Eight of those who die will be children. Every six

If today is an average day, eighty-two Americans will die from gunfire by midnight. Eight of those who die will be children.

hours of every day, a peace officer is fired upon. And every six days, one of those officers dies as a result.

With 240 million guns owned in the United States, we are fast approaching the point of one weapon for every man, woman, and child. And those guns result in more deaths in America than occur in all the major industrialized nations in the world combined: more than 29,000 a year. Nearly 3,000 are children who will never live to see their eighteenth birthdays.

The human toll, in terms of pain and suffering,

is staggering. For behind every single cold statistic is a tragic story of loss, leaving surviving loved ones to ask the unanswerable: Why? How can a single bullet, a cylinder of lead, often no larger than the end of a pencil, inflict damage so horrendous as to stop the human heart from beating, sever an artery, or turn the natural marvel of the brain into a useless mass?

And then there are colder numbers, reflecting the cost of this senseless violence: at last count, nearly $126 billion was spent trying to repair the bodies and minds that are torn apart by gunfire each year, placing an enormous burden on an already strained health care system.

A vivid illustration of the financial impact of gun violence was offered in a *Money* magazine article. The story focused on the impact of a forty-cent bullet fired from a twenty-dollar gun. The victim of the assault suffered a spinal cord injury and died one month later. His medical expenses totaled $65,000; life insurance benefits were $525,000; resultant Social Security and worker's compensation payments came to $46,000; criminal justice costs exceeded $200,000; and the price of lost productivity was $1,000,000, for a total cost of $1,836,000.

Who pays those costs? You do, through taxes and increased insurance premiums, at a time when the nation's fiscal resources are enormously strained and health care costs are skyrocketing out of control.

All the numbers, the tragic loss of life, the unwillingness to take governmental action, point to one inescapable conclusion: We do not have a gun problem in America. We have a gun epidemic, unprecedented and uncontrolled. Unlike the diseases for which cures are still sought, the means to dramatically reduce, to even halt, this deadly epidemic are known and within our grasp. Yet virtually every effort to reverse the deadly trend is resisted and, for the most part, stopped before it can begin.

> All the numbers, the tragic loss of life, the unwillingness to take governmental action, point to one inescapable conclusion: We do not have a gun problem in America. We have a gun epidemic, unprecedented and uncontrolled.

The problem—the epidemic—is not a new one. The bloodshed has been a tragic part of daily American life for as long as guns have been freely available and barely regulated.

But now a new and enormously troubling component of the problem has surfaced: terrorism.

There exists across America a chain of supermarkets of deadly weaponry, more than 4,000 of them, according to government reports, keeping doors open not only to legitimate users of firearms but also to weapons traffickers and to quantity buyers who seek to assemble illegal arsenals. How those arsenals can be, and already have been, used is frightening in the context of the war on terrorism that is being waged worldwide. Weapons bought at American

> Weapons bought at American gun shows have already been traced to suspected members of Al Qaeda, white supremacists, and the Irish Republican Army.

gun shows have already been traced to suspected members of Al Qaeda, white supremacists (including one who went on a murderous rampage against African Americans, Asians, and Jews), and the Irish Republican Army.

The will to end the bloodshed on our streets, in our homes, even in our schools, as well as to prevent the arming of terrorists, is not lacking among Americans. A clear majority of citizens supports such measures as banning assault weapons, mandating safe storage of firearms, and closing gun show loopholes that allow guns to flow freely into the hands of criminals. Yet that majority view is thwarted, year after year, by one of the most powerful lobbies in the nation: the gun lobby, funded by weapons and ammunition manufacturers and led by the powerful National Rifle Association.

Evidence of the power of that lobby came as recently as September 2004, when Congress refused to extend the assault weapons ban enacted ten years earlier to stop the manufacture of deadly rapid-fire guns that give criminals a clear firepower edge over police officers. With House and Senate elections less than two months off, members refused to even schedule votes on the extension. While there is no substantive proof of intimidation by the gun lobby, there is a sufficient record of members of Congress being defeated for reelection after campaigns were launched against them by the gun lobby.

Even the Federal Emergency Management Agency (FEMA) has been in the crosshairs of the NRA. Following the devastating Hurricane Katrina in 2005, FEMA made available to displaced residents of Louisiana an encampment of 600 trailers for temporary shelter. Because the trailers were very close together and were constructed with thin walls, a local sheriff's office asked FEMA to ban guns in the encampment as a safety precaution, citing the outbreaks of armed lawlessness in New Orleans following the hurricane. FEMA complied and, consequently, incurred immediate threats of lawsuits by the NRA and its ally, the Second Amendment Foundation. FEMA immediately backed down and said it would reconsider the firearms ban. As it turned out, law enforcement's fears were well founded: in the hurricane's aftermath, as panic and fear turned to violence, law and order broke down. While even some police officers, whose duty it was to protect the citizenry, took flight, guns were heard going off everywhere, adding to the panic and desperation, and innocent people died as a result. Once again, it was proved that when guns are added to the mix of disaster and hopelessness in the name of self-protection, law and order breaks down and the doors open to criminality.

NRA leader Wayne LaPierre made clear where the group stands when a choice is to be made between public safety and gun rights when he said, "Whether it's a national disaster, whether it's by nature like Katrina, or a flu pandemic, the Constitution can't be thrown out the window."

Still, there is the argument that nowhere does the Constitution say anything about safeguarding the rights of those who would seize upon a natural disaster to commit armed mayhem, to intimidate citizens, or to engage in looting at gunpoint.

> There are some defenders of absolute gun rights who actually believe that no one should be denied ownership of firearms, including convicted murderers, violent spousal abusers, the criminally insane, and even, incredible as it seems, potential terrorists.

This book will examine the scope of gun violence and explore its roots, including the much misused and misunderstood Second Amendment to the United States Constitution, which, gun supporters claim, grants to every American the absolute right to own and use all manner of firearms. Efforts continue to be made to clarify the amendment, which, many constitutional scholars believe, was intended only to ensure an armed militia during the nation's formative years, not to arm individuals to the hilt, regardless of criminal history, acts of domestic violence, or mental instability.

In short, there are some defenders of absolute gun rights who actually believe that no one should be denied ownership of firearms, including convicted murderers, violent spousal abusers, the criminally insane, and even, incredible as it seems, potential terrorists. These advocates of total, unfettered use of any and all sorts of deadly weapons would seem to condone the arming of the convicted murderer who is back on the streets again, the husband who continually beats his wife senseless and threatens to kill her,

> In an average three-week period, more Americans are killed by guns—in our homes, on our streets, in our public places—than all the U.S. soldiers killed in two years of war in Iraq.

the tortured soul whose paranoia drives him to destroy an authority figure, the substance abuser next door, the child molester, and those who would turn their hatred of America into terrorist acts against it. As the debate over gun violence continues to be waged in America, it becomes a question of whether we are willing to keep guns out of dangerous hands and allow them only in safe, responsible hands.

In a nation rightfully obsessed with ongoing international terrorism, there is an irony in the fact that, in an average three-week period, more Americans are killed by guns—in our homes, on our streets, in our public places—than all the U.S. soldiers killed in two years of war in Iraq.

Add to that the cold fact that ten times the number

of Americans die of gunshots each year than those killed in the 9/11 attack on our soil, and a grim picture of a deadly reign of domestic terror emerges. Like any form of terrorism, it takes its toll on people of all ages, colors, and economic backgrounds. Nearly half those deaths are self-inflicted by troubled people who choose guns to quickly and easily end their own lives. With newly developed weapons that can pierce any armored vest—weapons that can be legally purchased—police officers are in greater danger than ever before of being murdered as they do their jobs.

I hasten to add at this point that my deep concern over the gun violence epidemic in America is not born of a hatred of or opposition to firearms in and of themselves. To the contrary, I support legal and safe ownership and use of guns for legitimate purposes. I have used guns, both for sport and in my training while serving in the armed forces. I was a proud boy of eleven years when I was awarded both the marksman and sharpshooter badges in an NRA-sanctioned shooting program, which was the only condition under which I was allowed to fire a rifle.

But the NRA of my childhood is a far cry from the powerful industry lobby it has become today, making a mockery of reasonable efforts to stop the violence that grips the nation.

It is the obstructionism of the NRA and the violence spawned by irresponsible use of guns that I speak out against, violence that is, purely and simply, terrorism within our midst, homegrown and predictably deadly. Yet it is the one form of terror that can be prevented, with laws that can stop the flow of deadly weapons of destruction into the wrong hands.

The weekend gun show, a so-called American institution, has become a virtual bazaar for those bent on committing mayhem in our society. With but a few exceptions, a foreign terrorist can go to a suburban gun show on a peaceful Saturday morning and literally acquire an arsenal, with no questions asked, with which to go on a deadly rampage in a crowded mall, a public arena, or even a school filled with children.

> The weekend gun show, a so-called American institution, has become a virtual bazaar for those bent on committing mayhem in our society.

Cache of guns turns up in Pa. Murder case (Associated Press, November 17, 2005)
Lititz, Pa.—Police seized 54 guns from the home of an 18-year-old man charged with killing his girlfriend's parents and fleeing the state with her, according to court documents. … Police removed the collection of rifles, shotguns, handguns and ammunition Sunday from the home where David Ludwig lived with his parents. Neither of Ludwig's parents is licensed as a firearms dealer or collector, according to the national licensing

center of the federal Bureau of Alcohol,
Tobacco, Firearms and Explosives.

What could possibly have motivated the parents
of an eighteen-year-old to store more than fifty
deadly weapons in their home, where the young man
could simply take one of his choice to kill the parents
of his fourteen-year-old girlfriend because the parents did not approve of the relationship?

Will the carnage ever stop? Only if and when the
majority views of the American public are acted
upon with such simple remedies as requiring background checks for all gun purchases, in all venues,
and with all transactions, whether in stores, gun
shows, over the back fence, or out of the trunks of
cars; reinstating the federal ban on deadly assault
weapons; requiring safe storage of all guns in the
home; and holding the gun industry accountable for
the death and destruction caused by the products it
manufactures and markets.

In fact, the majority views call for even more-
restrictive measures than are currently proposed by
such advocacy groups as the Brady Campaign to
Prevent Gun Violence.

A study of American attitudes toward guns and
violence was conducted in 1999 by the National
Opinion Research Center at the University of Chicago
in collaboration with the John Hopkins Center for
Gun Policy and Research. Following are verbatim
excerpts from that study:

- Three-fourths of gun owners support mandatory registration of handguns, as does 85 percent of the general public.
- Two-thirds of gun owners and 80 percent of the general public favor mandatory background checks in private handgun sales, such as gun shows.
- When asked if there should be a mandatory background check and a five-day waiting period in order to purchase a gun, 82 percent of the people owning a gun, as well as 85 percent of the general public, agreed that position was a good idea.

Clearly, the results of this survey indicate that the American public understands the need to strengthen this nation's gun policies. People readily accept strong regulation of the manufacture, sale, and distribution of these dangerous consumer products. Still, the intransigence of the gun lobby is unprecedented and continues in opposition to the will of the majority of Americans. Unlike the tobacco, asbestos, and automotive industries, the manufacturers of deadly firearms have not only refused to accept

> The manufacturers of deadly firearms have not only refused to accept any culpability for the deadly guns they make, but they have now succeeded in convincing the U.S. Congress to grant them immunity from civil liability.

any culpability for the deadly guns they make, but they have now succeeded in convincing the U.S. Congress to grant them immunity from civil liability. This is the only American industry that makes products whose purpose is to kill, yet it has been singled out for immunity from liability by both houses of Congress with a lobbyist-supported bill that was happily signed into law by the president.

Makers of cigarettes have had to face liability for the deaths their products have caused; auto and tire manufacturers have been held financially accountable for death and injury resulting from use of their products; even companies that produce bunk beds and flannel pajamas are held liable for accidental deaths caused by the goods they make. Unlike firearms, none of the products of those industries are designed to kill, but when they do cause death or maim users, civil actions result in punitive judgments. Only the industry that makes and sells products that are deadly by design is given a free pass from liability by a Congress and a president that bend to the will of an all-powerful, and generally feared, gun lobby.

Why is this unbridled power of a special interest, this lack of courage in the legislative and executive branches of our government, allowed to subvert the will of the people of America while the mayhem continues to spread throughout the nation?

That is a question that confounds those Americans of conscience who are daily waging a war against gun violence. For now, those who fight the good battle are in the minority in the Congress. Yet people whose interests they are supposed to represent constitute a clear majority supporting more gun control. It is a disparity that begs to be reversed. When the gun lobby succeeds in bullying politicians into killing one of the more important laws enacted to curb gun violence—the assault weapons ban—it was a vote against citizens' best interests. And, just months later, when that same lobby brought enough pressure to bear to grant unprecedented immunity to the gun industry, the people's best interests were once again subverted to the will of the NRA, which purports to represent the interests of hunting sportsmen and -women, when, in fact, only a small minority of legitimate gun owners are even members.

Coupled with the bullying tactics of the arms industry is what can only be called a short public memory of tragedies that have been seminal in the gun safety movement. When there is a massacre like Columbine, people are outraged at the insanity that allows children to illegally acquire deadly weapons with which they kill innocent people and then themselves. When two snipers kill passersby randomly in and around the nation's capital, there is again outrage. But then time passes. People forget the anguish of every parent, spouse, and friend who also falls victim to the senseless bloodshed. And the forces against sensible regulation of guns seize on the fading memories to advance their agenda again.

What will it take to keep those dark memories in the forefront of America's conscience? Another terrible tragedy in a school, on a commuter train, or on a freeway?

Will it only end when a band of terrorists who manage to penetrate our borders go to gun shows and legally amass a cache of weapons with the ability to shoot down an airliner, or penetrate the armor plate of a National Guard tank on an American street, or pierce a supposedly bulletproof vest of a police officer?

In the name of the eighty-two Americans, including the eight children, who will die of gun violence today, let us hope the answer is no.

It is to those victims—the innocent, the young, the troubled—that this book is dedicated, with an abiding hope for change.

Chapter 2
When Voices Are Louder Than Gunfire

It started with a phone call that came on Saturday, May 1, 1999, ten days after the Columbine massacre, when Charlton Heston addressed the annual NRA convention in Denver.

"This is John Head. I'm in Washington, but I heard about what went on in Denver today." He was referring to the protest by thousands of citizens of the NRA's refusal to call off a fiery speech by Heston so soon after Columbine. "You know, we've got to do something about this gun violence. It's gotten out of hand."

John is a friend of more than twenty years. He is a well-known Denver attorney specializing in class action suits. We have always enjoyed good-natured political sparring; he is a lifelong Republican and I a committed Democrat. Our party differences have never gotten in the way of friendship. Now they were about to serve us and an idea we held for stopping the violence.

"Somebody needs to take on the NRA," he continued.

Just hours earlier, I had said exactly the same

words to a longtime political activist who attended the protest.

"How do we do it? They're the most powerful lobby in the country," I reminded John.

"It's got to be bipartisan. Democrats, like you, Republicans, like me. It's the only way it's going to work."

And he was right. We agreed that evening to start a grassroots movement to challenge the gun lobby, to prove that Colorado, which has always been considered a gun-friendly frontier state, knew better than to allow the gun carnage to continue unchecked.

Two days later, we formed an organization named, by John, SAFE Colorado (Sane Alternative to the Firearms Epidemic). One week later, we had a board of directors and two co-chairmen whose political affiliations were equally divided between the two parties. John and I became co-presidents. And, never having lobbied for anything or formed a nonprofit organization, we put our heads down and plowed ahead, vowing to change the laws that allow guns to pass so easily into the hands of murderers.

The first phone call we made was to Richard Lamm, former three-term Democratic governor of Colorado. He agreed to be one of our co-chairs. We told him we needed to balance him with a Republican. Before the day was out, he had enlisted another former governor, John Love, who had also served as President Richard Nixon's energy czar, to be the other co-chair.

For the board of directors, we applied the same bipartisan standard: each Democrat appointed had to be accompanied by a Republican, in matched pairs. We also excluded current political officeholders or candidates for office to ensure against possible conflicts of interest.

We began with J. D. MacFarlane, former Colorado attorney general, a Democrat, matched with Mary Estill Buchanan, one-time Colorado secretary of state and Republican candidate for the U.S. Senate against Gary Hart. The irony of that pairing was that MacFarlane and Buchanan served at the same time and were constant political adversaries in the 1970s; now they shared a common mission and only infrequently did they lock horns in political debate in SAFE meetings.

Finally, Rabbi Steven Foster of Denver's Temple Emanuel, known for his advocacy of civil and women's rights, was seated on the board together with David Sprecace, an attorney active in the state Republican Party.

Now we had a board and two high-profile chairs, evenly balanced politically, and, most important of all, an unswerving commitment to doing what had not been done in Colorado before: taking up a slingshot, we liked to say; David against the gun lobby Goliath. On May 10, 1999, we publicly announced the formation of SAFE Colorado along with our mission to beat the NRA at its own game.

In the weeks following Columbine, the Colorado

legislature had been thrown into a state of turmoil, first over a package of bills that had been introduced before the massacre, which included a ban on cities' rights to sue gun manufacturers, a bill to allow carrying concealed handguns in public, and a prohibition of local limits and controls of firearms. All the bills, which were backed by the gun lobby and seemed destined for passage by the Republican-controlled legislature, were hurriedly withdrawn in the wake of Columbine.

Next, Republican Governor Bill Owens presented his own package of recommended bills, all of which placed restrictions on gun sales and were vehemently opposed by the gun lobby, which openly attacked Owens, previously considered an ally, as a turncoat.

It was at that point that the board of SAFE decided to retain a lobbyist to work in the legislature on our behalf, trying to convince members to vote for the new bills offered by Owens. We approached the one person whom we felt would be most convincing, someone who had never lobbied before, someone who was already publicly advocating for new gun controls and knew firsthand the devastation of gun violence: Tom Mauser. It took a fair amount of convincing to get Tom to join us. He worried that his family, still in a state of shock over their loss in the Columbine tragedy, where their son, Daniel, was killed, might be troubled by the publicity that he would attract in the controversial debate. Finally, though, Tom agreed that there was much to be gained by his presence in the movement, a presence that he also agreed would serve as a tribute to Daniel's memory, and he became our legislative representative.

The governor's package had included requiring background checks for private sales at gun shows (closing the gun show loophole, in effect), mandating safe storage of firearms, and setting the minimum age for handgun purchases at twenty-one. The entire package eventually failed in the legislature, leaving Colorado with no new regulations that could work to prevent future Columbines.

That is where our new organization stepped in to try to achieve what the legislature refused to achieve, by vowing to take the gun violence issue to the people.

After announcing our plans for a statewide referendum, we were contacted by Brian Malte, an executive with Handgun Control, Inc., now known as the Brady Campaign to Prevent Gun Violence, in Washington, D.C.

"We've been reading about you folks out there in Colorado. And we're interested in helping you with your efforts," said Malte, a young man of boundless energy and an intense commitment to the cause of stopping the violence. "How about coming back here to our national meeting and seeing what we can do to help?"

John Head and I accepted and went to Washington for three days of meetings, seminars, and strategy sessions attended by groups similar to ours from across the nation. It was an intense short course in taking on the gun lobby and advocating for sensible gun laws.

Brian gave us sound advice: "Don't try to do too much at once; work incrementally for progress; choose the most important issue of all for the people of Colorado."

As a result, we took to the board a recommendation to put the one issue that could have made a difference before Columbine—closing the gun show loophole—to a statewide vote of the people. No other state in the nation had tried to close the loophole by requiring background checks for all sales, whether by licensed dealers or private sellers.

The next step in the genesis of SAFE came at the airport in Washington while we waited in a lounge for our return flight to Denver wondering what we could do to attract more interest in our fledgling organization and to involve young people.

"What if we were to bring a bunch of kids back here to Washington to talk to people in Congress, to put pressure on them to do something about guns?" I asked John.

As has always been typical of John, he said nothing but merely nodded as he dialed a number on his cell phone. No response to my suggestion. No discussion. I thought he might be calling his office or his home. He dialed another number and then I heard him say, "This is John Head calling. I'd like to speak to someone about chartering an airplane."

He soon was negotiating space on a United

Airlines flight to Washington for a trip he wanted to make as soon as possible, he told whomever was on the other end of the line. That was his way of letting me know he liked the idea and wanted to move ahead with it.

One month later, in July 1999, we were taking ninety-nine young people—mainly high school students, many of whom attended Columbine, and some college students—to Washington for two days of witnessing the legislative process, lobbying senators and representatives for federal gun controls, and for an experience that no one on the trip, including those of us who chaperoned, is likely to ever forget: a private meeting with President Bill Clinton in the White House.

One of our chaperones was Dottie Lamm, former first lady of Colorado and passionate advocate of sensible gun laws. We were given free accommodations at a George Washington University dormitory, where Dottie served as everything from housemother to seminar leader to simply a good and trusted friend of the students.

We were informed by White House staffers that the meeting with the president was scheduled for forty-five minutes. When the scheduled time was up, someone made a signal to the president to remind him. He replied, grinning broadly, "They're telling me the time's up. But I'm having too good a time. Let's keep going." And he and the students did just that for another half-hour.

There is something about the grandeur of the White House that can easily intimidate anyone—anyone except, perhaps, a young man from the inner city of Denver, who was first on his feet when the president asked for questions following his remarks to the group.

"Mr. President," said the young man, bobbing back and forth as he stood, displaying just a touch of the hip-hop style. "You've been talking about how terrible it was at Columbine, with all those shootings. Hey, I agree. It was real bad. But, Mr. President, that's been going on all the time where I live, in my neighborhood, you know what I'm saying? What are you going to do about that?"

Most of the adults in the room held our breath, certain that the young man had breached protocol. President Clinton looked down, listening to every word intently, nodding his head. Then he looked up at the young man and spoke. "You know, you're absolutely right. You've been living with violence too long. So I'm going to make a promise to you today. When I'm in Denver again, I will go to your neighborhood to see what we can do, together, to stop the violence, to end the fear. And I want to thank you for bringing that up."

John and I exchanged looks of relief. And in my heart, I knew we had done the right thing, that we had come to the right place and brought the right people to do something about gun violence in America.

After the meeting, the president, along with

Attorney General Janet Reno, took the entire student group outside and stood with them to hold a press conference heavily attended by national and international media. He made certain to make the Colorado students the stars of the event, and he repeated his promise to work for ending the gun violence that was taking so heavy a toll on America's youth.

Back in Denver, we set about on our mission to grow our organization, raise funds for our efforts, and begin plans for placing an initiative on the November 2000 ballot to close the gun show loophole.

We also formed a students' organization, SAFE Students of Colorado, to be headed by two young activists, Ben Gelt and David Winkler, who had been instrumental in forming the group we took to Washington and who also worked tirelessly to involve students across Colorado and in other states as well.

On April 12, 2000, we launched our effort to get the initiative, which became known as Amendment 22, on the ballot. It became an even more auspicious event than we had planned when President Clinton kept his promise to come to Denver and work to end the violence. To a capacity crowd in Denver's convention center, with gun rights protestors clamoring behind police lines outside, and standing beneath a banner proclaiming "CLOSE THE GUN SHOW LOOPHOLE. SAVE THE CHILDREN," the president delivered a stirring speech, urging everyone there to get a petition and get out the message to take a historic step forward in behalf of a safer state and nation and to honor the memory of those who died at Columbine.

We were told by the Colorado secretary of state that some 62,000 valid signatures were required to get the initiative on the ballot. It seemed like a large number to us until we saw the enormous turnout of petition carriers who went out on the streets and into the shopping centers to launch the drive. Unlike most ballot efforts, we did not use paid signature gatherers. It was not merely a matter of economy; it was one of principle. We were a grassroots organization; our people would work long and hard out of passion for an issue, not for a paycheck.

I knew we would prevail that first spring evening of the drive following a launching press conference at which Governor Owens, Mayor Webb, Colorado Attorney General Ken Salazar, and Denver District Attorney Bill Ritter were the first four petition signers.

When I went to a suburban supermarket at 9:00 P.M. to check on how things were going the first day, I approached a woman who appeared to be in her seventies holding a stack of petitions and looking weary but smiling proudly.

How long had she been out there? Eight hours at least, she guessed. How many signatures had she gathered? She waved a heavy stack of completed forms, holding hundreds of signatures. She had not had time to count, she said. When I asked her if she were ready to go home, she said, "Are you kidding? The store's still open. I'm not going anywhere."

On the day in August when petitions were to be

submitted to the secretary of state, we held a rally on the steps of the state capitol. Were we turning in the required 62,000 signatures? No. We had gathered more than 100,000, nearly double the number necessary, just for good measure.

Now we were officially on the ballot. Next came the community forums, the speakers' bureaus, the debates with those who opposed the effort. We retained the services of a renowned political consultant considered to be the dean of political lobbyists, former political science professor Wally Stealy. He guided us though a statewide television and newspaper advertising campaign. Two commercials, which ran repeatedly in all major state markets, portrayed ten young schoolchildren, singing "America the Beautiful" in unison. Every few seconds, however, one of the children would disappear from the screen, along with his or her voice, until only one child remained, singing the last line alone. Then she too disappeared, leaving ten empty chairs, while an announcer said, "Every day in America, ten children die in gun violence. We can stop that … by closing the gun show loophole. Vote yes on 22." (Since the airing of that commercial, the number of child deaths has dropped, thankfully, from ten to eight for the last reporting year, which is still eight too many.)

On November 7, 2000, history was made in Colorado. The initiative to close the gun show loophole passed by an overwhelming majority, with more than 70 percent of the vote. The people of this so-called frontier, gun-friendly state showed that it was also a reasonable, child-friendly state. In spite of the rancor, the attempts at intimidating our staff and members, the cries of police state tactics, the veiled threats against us, the name-calling, the people spoke.

Something was proved that day. A question was answered: how can we beat the NRA? Seventeen thousand people, the membership of SAFE Colorado, showed exactly how it can be done.

Chapter 3
Sarah's Fight

What was it in the development of this nation that led us to become the most heavily armed nation in the world?

I asked that question of Sarah Brady, chair of the Brady Campaign to Prevent Gun Violence. Her answer was simple, to the point, and certainly provocative: "We haven't grown up yet," said this tireless fighter of senseless gun violence.

Sarah is a woman who has earned her credentials to speak out on the issue of gun violence and to condemn those forces that block the solutions available to stem the deadly tide. Her husband, Jim, just barely survived an assassin's bullet when twenty-six-year-old John Hinckley tried to kill President Ronald Reagan on March 30, 1981. Hinckley's motive was admittedly not political (in a bizarre show of bipartisanship, he had stalked President Carter in 1980 but did not carry out his assassination plan).

Hinckley is a classic case of a person who should never have been allowed to own or use a gun. He had a history of mental illness. His motive for stalking

Carter and shooting Reagan was a twisted one: to impress actress Jodie Foster, with whom he had become obsessed and whom he stalked for more than a year. His assassination attempt, by his own admission, was intended to impress the actress, to gain her respect.

Prior to the attack on President Reagan, the delusional Hinckley was treated for depression and was prescribed tranquilizers and antidepressants. Yet, in spite of his mental state, he was able to buy a .38-caliber pistol, as well as exploding-head Devastator bullets that he eventually used in his attack on Reagan, one of which smashed into the skull of then–press secretary Jim Brady. Reagan fully recovered from his wound, but Jim Brady, who had at one point been listed as a fatality, valiantly clung to life for days and eventually survived, though unable to ever walk again, and, to this day, he remains confined to a wheelchair. Although the brain damage placed limits on Jim Brady's mobility, he, along with his wife, Sarah, has become a tireless advocate for reasonable gun laws under the auspices of the two organizations named for them, the Brady Center to Prevent Gun Violence and the Brady Campaign to Prevent Gun Violence.

In spite of the horror of the attempt on Ronald

> In spite of his mental state, he (Hinckley) was able to buy a .38-caliber pistol, as well as exploding-head Devastator bullets that he eventually used in his attack on Reagan.

Reagan's life, there still remain today forces that advocate for the ability of someone like John Hinckley to own and use deadly firearms. Why? Because he has a "right" to do so, supposedly under the Second Amendment, according to the more extreme gun rights advocates. Such thinking lends credence to Sarah Brady's view that America has yet to grow up, at least in regard to the gun violence issue.

Perhaps one of the reasons there is not more revulsion at the kind of senseless violence that struck down Jim Brady is the extent to which society has become inured to deadly weapons and their deadly toll. All it takes is a trip to the movies or an evening in front of a television set to see how sanitized the horrific power of a bullet has become. Impressionable children watch crime shows or films and see a gun fired at a villain or at a police officer, resulting in a loud pop, a cry of simulated pain, and the familiar red blot of imitation blood staining a white shirt.

Generations of Westerns portray guns blazing and people falling over, often getting up again and riding off on horses. Good guys shoot bad guys, who usually go down easily, and bad guys shoot good guys, who don't seem to be especially fazed by a slug

Perhaps one of the reasons there is not more revulsion at the kind of senseless violence that struck down Jim Brady is the extent to which society has become inured to deadly weapons and their deadly toll.

of lead crashing into a shoulder, a leg, or a torso.

Is it any wonder that a child levels a finger at a playmate, shouts "bang," and waits for the friend to double over and fall down before getting back up, brushing himself off, and moving painlessly on to something else?

No. *Because we haven't grown up.*

Like so many activists in the gun violence prevention movement, the Bradys were thrust into the issue by personal tragedy. Prior to the day that changed the course of their lives so dramatically, Jim was thriving in a high-pressure job as spokesman for the Reagan White House. Sarah, who had worked on the staffs of two members of Congress, was raising their son, Scott, and staying involved in Republican Party politics. Gun violence was not constantly on either of their minds, yet the growing number of senseless firearm deaths had always been a concern they shared with many Americans.

Sarah agreed to an interview for this book in October 2005, although she was still recovering from recent surgery.

She is an attractive and vital middle-aged woman with a professional air, a genial smile, and eyes that bespeak her total approachability. In the lobby of her hotel, she looked at home among what appeared to be a political crowd, as is the case in most upscale hotels in Washington. She could easily have passed for a congresswoman or, at the very least, the influential lobbyist she is, the face and voice of the Brady Campaign and Center, as well as the Million Mom March, in her ongoing effort to reduce gun violence in America.

The evening following the interview, Sarah was an honored guest at a fund-raising gala, proceeds from which went to the Brady Campaign. The event was held at the French Embassy and celebrated the eightieth birthday of syndicated columnist Art Buchwald, a longtime supporter of gun regulation (and, coincidentally, a proud World War II veteran of the U.S. Marine Corps; the most moving moment of the evening for Buchwald was when he stood to hear "From the Halls of Montezuma" sung to him).

It was hard to miss the irony of Sarah arriving at the event and having to enter through a gauntlet of protestors called the Tyranny Response Team, dressed in tricornered hats and knickers and looking more like they were on their way to a costume party than to make a political counterpoint. The TRT is active wherever there are efforts to legislate gun safety measures. They sometimes march outside gun safety events with drummers beating out some sort of patriotic, solemn warning that gun regulation of any kind is a threat to America's freedom.

"I've always been on the side of some types of gun control," said Sarah. "I grew up in a family where it was common sense."

Her father, Stan Kemp, was a career FBI agent, and gun safety was a given in the family's home in Arlington, Virginia.

"Every night, when my father came home from work, the first thing he would do was go upstairs, take off his revolver, and lock it away. He hated the idea of carrying the gun when he was off duty, which he had to do as part of his job as an agent in a field office. He just wasn't a gun lover at all."

Has Sarah ever fired a gun?

"Oh, yes. When I was little I went to the FBI firing range and shot. Actually, I shot a machine gun and some other type of long gun. Then I didn't shoot a gun for many, many years. And then when my son was about twelve, he had a friend who regularly went hunting with his father. And Scott kept wanting to learn to shoot a gun. I'd never bought him a play gun or anything like that. By this time I was already involved in the gun issue. My feeling was if he was going to shoot, then let's do it right. So we went on a vacation to the Homestead, where they had a range and offered instruction. We both shot .22 rifles. And I actually enjoyed it. It was a challenge, like shooting pool. Look, I'm not anti-gun. I can understand someone enjoying shooting at a target. It wasn't a human being."

Her husband, Jim, was the first human being in Sarah's world to become a target.

When it happened, their lives changed as quickly as the hundredth of a second it takes for a bullet to travel from the muzzle of a pistol to the skull of an innocent victim.

The anger at the injustice of the shooting of Jim Brady erupted one day from the lips of three-year-old

Scott, who had become frustrated with the fatigue he saw overtaking his mother, consuming her.

In her book, *A Good Fight*, Sarah recounts one evening when she was totally exhausted from the rigors of caring for Jim, yet still taking the time to read a book to her son. She noticed the child wasn't paying attention, seeming preoccupied. When Sarah suggested it was bedtime and he needed to settle down, he started to cry.

"I hate John Hinckley, I hate John Hinckley!" he blurted out.

Sarah was shocked, because that name had been purposely avoided in the Brady home, for obvious reasons.

"Honey, why?" asked Sarah. "We don't hate anyone."

He replied, "Well if John Hinckley hadn't shot Daddy, then you wouldn't be so tired all the time."

Sarah just lay there with Scott in the bed and the two of them cried together until he finally fell asleep.

"It was a real expiation, I guess, for both of us," says Sarah. "He was so little, yet so understanding."

It turned out to be only the first expiation to follow Jim's shooting. There would be more to come, perhaps the most significant of which was the passage, in November 1993, of the Brady Bill, named for Jim and Sarah's efforts to stop gun violence in America. The bill was signed into law by President Bill Clinton in the face of enormous opposition by the NRA and in spite of a vigorous filibuster effort

led by then-senator Bob Dole, who has often identified himself with the gun lobby.

The bill was far more than a symbolic gesture in
the crusade to reverse the increase of gun violence. It
initially mandated a five-day waiting period for buyers of firearms from licensed dealers and required a
national criminal background check on those buyers.
A provision that required local law enforcement officials to perform the background checks was struck
down by the Supreme Court in 1998. But in place of
local checks, the FBI developed the National Instant
Criminal Background Check System (NICS), which
remains in place today. Simply stated, the Brady
Bill is designed to keep deadly firearms out of the
wrong hands, the hands of those who would use
guns to kill, injure, or commit acts of terror.
Among those who are denied gun purchases are convicted felons, domestic
abusers, and those illegally in the United States.

> The Brady Bill is designed to keep deadly firearms out of the wrong hands, the hands of those who would use guns to kill, injure, or commit acts of terror.

Yet to this day, the gun lobby still rails against
the Brady Bill, calling it everything from the "start
down the slippery slope to gun confiscation," to a
subversive plot against gun owners, to nothing more
than a "feel-good law."

But statistics tell a different story, one that belies
the notion of simply feeling good or confiscating guns.

According to the FBI's National Crime Information Center (NCIC) reporting in 2002, more than half a million—563,000—gun purchases were refused in the eight years following NCIC's inception. During a similar period, with the Brady Bill and background checks in force, gun deaths declined 27 percent, from 39,595 in 1993 to 28,874 in 2001. And virtually all denials of purchase were to convicted felons or persons indicted on felony charges.

> With the Brady Bill and background checks in force, gun deaths declined 27 percent, from 39,595 in 1993 to 28,874 in 2001. And virtually all denials of purchase were to convicted felons or persons indicted on felony charges.

Given those numbers, is the Brady Bill merely a feel-good law, a step down the slippery slope to taking guns away from law-abiding buyers and users, or has it helped reduced markedly the daily slaughter by guns in the wrong hands?

As the saying goes, "Do the math."

Sarah and Jim Brady have done more than work for the Brady Bill, although that achievement alone is hailed by gun violence prevention advocates as a historic achievement in and of itself. The couple continues to travel the country in support of local prevention efforts, speaking to citizen groups, lobbying for additional laws they see as further reducing the firearms toll, and, of course, challenging the gun lobby for its refusal to acknowledge the success of laws like Brady.

In a message to Brady Campaign and Center members, Jim and Sarah recently said, "We have been in this fight for nearly twenty-five years, and whenever we find ourselves discouraged, we take heart in knowing that the American people are on our side. The law enforcement community is on our side. And families throughout this country who have lost loved ones to gun violence are on our side."

Showing their willingness to face adversaries head on, they continued, "This issue is bigger than the politics in Washington. It's about fathers and mothers, sons and daughters who are losing their lives needlessly because our leaders in Congress and the administration won't stand up to the special interests of the gun lobby. It's a fight worth fighting, and we will never quit."

What are the battles that still need to be waged? An obvious one is the reinstatement of the assault weapons ban, which the Congress allowed to die in the 2005 session. There were not enough votes in the Republican-controlled

> "This issue is bigger than the politics in Washington. It's about fathers and mothers, sons and daughters who are losing their lives needlessly because our leaders in Congress and the administration won't stand up to the special interests of the gun lobby. It's a fight worth fighting, and we will never quit."
> —Sarah Brady

legislative branch to keep the ban on deadly assault weapons in place—a victory for the powerful arms lobby, a defeat for a frustrated coalition of gun violence–control advocates, not just Brady and Million Mom March members, but those who are daily in the line of fire: police officers.

"We've been working on that issue since the 1980s," said Sarah. "Part of the problem was calling it an assault weapons ban." She has been in the movement long enough to understand the problem of semantics in advocating for gun regulations.

"Ban," she pointed out, is a negative word, one that the gun lobby seizes upon all too readily, claiming it is proof that proponents are, in fact, trying to take all guns away from everyone. Opponents are reluctant to admit that the intent of the ban is simply to keep powerful, deadly weapons available only to the military and law enforcement and unavailable to private citizens. But, as is often the case in the rhetoric of such controversy, words have power. And opponents of banning assault weapons claim it is tantamount to confiscation of existing guns. The truth is, though, that only new sales of such weapons and of those in production would be prohibited; previously sold weapons would not be affected.

The late John Love, who served as Republican governor of Colorado and also as Richard Nixon's energy czar, was an avid hunter. When, following the Columbine massacre, he was approached to serve as SAFE Colorado's co-chairman, he remarked, "I've got several guns. I love to hunt with them. But what do people need those damn assault weapons for? To shoot a deer or a pheasant?"

"The problem with assault weapons isn't how they look," said Sarah. "I don't care how they look. They can be just as ugly as hell, as long as they don't have high-capacity magazines, and won't accept them, and aren't fingerprint proof."

Sarah believes the best effort to reduce the threat of assault weapons is to treat them in a way similar to the ways cars are regulated.

"Let's set up regulations instead of bans. We have standards and regulations for automobiles. It's not a first step to banning automobiles. It's public safety."

In assessing the problems currently facing advocacy groups such as Brady, Sarah referred to a major setback that was occurring at the time of the interview: the Gun Industry Immunity Bill, which had easily passed the Senate and was sure to win passage by the House as well as receive George Bush's promised signature into law. The same bill was easily defeated in 2004, thanks to concerted efforts by Brady and other lobbying forces, but the NRA brought enormous pressure to bear in 2005, pressure that was not resisted by the Republicans in control of the Congress and the White House, who seemed determined to reward their gun industry friends with an unprecedented free pass from civil accountability in the courts.

"With the Immunity Bill, which is going to take away the ability of victims to sue, I suspect we're going to see gun manufacturers really pushing the type of weaponry to the limit. We're going to start seeing some really weird guns out there now. The ban isn't there anymore, and with immunity we're going to see the gunmakers really emboldened, flooding the markets with every kind of gun they want to sell, regardless of the danger."

I asked Sarah what she thought could and should have been done to prevent the kind of tragedy that struck her husband down in the assassination attempt.

"There's certainly a chance a background check would have prevented Hinckley from getting a gun. When he had been stalking President Carter, his first target, he tried to buy a gun in Tennessee. But there was a two-week waiting period in force there. So he traveled to Texas, where he knew he could get a gun without a mandated waiting period. In those days, you were supposed to buy a gun in the state where you lived. So he lied about his residence on his application form. And he got his gun illegally. If Texas had run a background check, they likely would have caught him in his lie and denied him the purchase."

> "With the Immunity Bill, which is going to take away the ability of victims to sue, I suspect … we're going to see the gunmakers really emboldened, flooding the markets with every kind of gun they want to sell, regardless of the danger."
> —Sarah Brady

Referring again to the dubious distinction the

United States holds as the most violent of all the industrialized nations combined, Sarah used words such as "arrogance" and "frontier mentality."

"Other countries, in Europe especially, have learned over the years that there are certain ways to get along with one another, to resolve conflict. Maybe that's simply because they're a lot older than we are. It could be that we're still a young and spoiled country."

Is there a chance that America will change its ways and become less violent in the future?

"I think we're becoming more and more civilized as time goes on. Just look at every aspect of our arrogance. We're almost like an eighteen-year-old whippersnapper in contrast to a more mature fifty-year-old. It especially showed after World War II. We finally won that war. We had a boom here, after going through the depression before that. I remember in the sixties, when I traveled abroad and we started hearing about the ugly American over there. I guess we had an arrogance. I myself went to Europe thinking the Dutch still wore those funny wooden shoes and just made cheese and Switzerland was just cuckoo clocks. What a shock it was to get over there and find out how sophisticated everyone was. And I guess when a country is around long enough to be mature, to be sophisticated, it's probably going to be less prone to violence."

Why did America develop with very different attitudes toward guns from those held by the mother country, England?

"We were settled by people who very unhappy with restrictions they had lived with in England. They came here and wanted freedom, complete and total freedom to do what they wanted to do. The East Coast grew and became more civilized, and restrictions developed in places like Massachusetts and New York, not just about guns, but things like zoning and taxation that people felt were encroachment on freedoms. So they began to move westward. Which is why I think the West does the least in terms of limits on guns."

> "There should be clear distinctions between guns that should be made available to the public and those that should not. But the gun industry doesn't want to establish those differences."
> —Sarah Brady

What kind of additional restraints should be placed on firearms?

"I think we ought to have restrictions on the manufacture of weapons, on matters of reliability and safety. I see no purpose for guns like the .50-calibre machine gun, except for use by the armed forces and law enforcement. There should be clear distinctions between guns that should be made available to the public and those that should not. But the gun industry doesn't want to establish those differences."

The .50-calibre machine gun Sarah referred to is perhaps the most devastating weapon made that can still be considered a firearm, as opposed to artillery, such as mortars, cannons, and rockets. It can pierce an inch-thick steel armor plate—or, more easily, a so-called bulletproof vest worn by police officers. I can personally attest to the power of what's called the "50-cal" in gun parlance; while in basic aviation training in the U.S. Navy, I fired one. But it had to be bolted down to concrete, so strong was its explosive power. Yet the weapon can be bought at most gun shows. Someone with enough money can amass a devastating armory of those weapons and wage a mini-war against police on duty, civilians at a sporting event, or workers coming out of an office building.

> Someone with enough money can amass a devastating armory of those weapons and wage a mini-war against police on duty, civilians at a sporting event, or workers coming out of an office building.

Once again, the gun lobby does not deem the 50-cal too dangerous to be owned by private citizens. It becomes increasingly difficult to imagine that America's founding fathers had a weapon like that in mind when they established the right of citizens to arm themselves in the Bill of Rights.

To show the absurdity of the NRA's misappropriation of the Bill of Rights to justify private ownership of weapons of destruction, some gun regulation advocates have suggested, not without irony, that the Second Amendment should continue to guarantee the right of a citizen to own any and all guns that were available in the year 1789, when the right was established. Which would mean anyone could buy and keep a long flintlock rifle that had to be loaded with a ball, a small powder bag, and tamped with a ramrod before being fired. Imagine, they say, someone trying to hijack a car, hold up a convenience store, or commit suicide with a blunderbuss.

Another of Jim and Sarah Brady's goals, in addition to reinstating assault weapon restrictions, is extension of federally mandated criminal background checks at gun shows to cover all gun purchases, whether from a licensed dealer or by private sale.

Under the present system, only those guns offered for sale by federally licensed dealers are subject to NCIC background checks. That means that the hundreds of thousands of transactions that are conducted at gun shows, swap meets, through classified ads, or simply "over the back fence" do not require background checks, except in states such as Colorado and Oregon, which passed laws designed to close the loophole, precisely the kind of loophole that allowed three of the weapons used in the Columbine massacre to pass into the hands of the young killers.

The inconsistencies that currently exist in laws governing sales at gun shows in most states create dangerous opportunities for criminals and terrorists to avoid compliance with existing federal laws regarding age, criminality, and history of violence.

An example of how easy it is to pass through those loopholes: Two teenagers working in the gun-violence control movement before Colorado closed the loopholes went to a weekend gun show to see just how many and what kind of firearms they could buy without proving their age or that they were not felons.

They systematically approached vendors who were not licensed dealers, many of whom posted signs such as "NOT A LICENSED DEALER," the signal that they could conduct no-questions-asked sales. Within less than an hour, the two teens were offered everything from semiautomatic weapons to kits that can modify those weapons into fully automatic (and totally illegal) machine guns.

The young men even asked if they needed to show a driver's license or any other proof of eligibility to buy guns. Their questions were met with cynical smiles and firm reassurances that such matters were of no concern.

As one of the young men later said, "We could have walked out of there with enough firepower to commit several Columbines."

Whether the Bradys will see a national background check enacted is uncertain, at best, given the gun lobby's vow to never acquiesce to such a law. But that will not stop Sarah and Jim from continuing to wage the battle that could create a system that, had it been in place at the time, could have prevented a bullet from tearing into Jim's brain and nearly assassinating an American president—again. Sarah also hopes for reversal of the immunity granted the gun industry under the 2005 NRA-backed bill.

"It's ridiculous to give that kind of total avoidance

of accountability to an industry that makes such deadly products," she said.

Part of the problem in reversing the total immunity for the industry, said Sarah, is the disdain with which many Americans view lawsuits and the lawyers who file them.

"People just don't like the idea of lawsuits—until, of course, they need one for themselves," she said. "So we have to find ways to convince the American people that manufacturers must be held liable for products they make that are designed to kill people."

The issue of products that are deadly by design, and yet whose manufacturers cannot be held accountable for what they do to people, is glaringly inconsistent with the long-standing concept of product liability that prevails in this country. Products made by other industries, such as automobiles, cigarettes, and alcohol, also figure in deaths. But the difference is that those products are not designed to cause death; when they do, their manufacturers and marketers can be held accountable in the courts. Additionally, cars, tobacco, and alcohol are far more regulated than firearms.

In pressing for the Immunity Bill, Sarah acknowledges that the gun lobby was able to capitalize on perceptions of a too litigious society. "People have a misconception about lawsuits," she says. "They have the idea that most lawsuits against companies are frivolous. They think someone's suing McDonald's every day over getting burned by coffee, but it just doesn't happen. On top of that, they constantly hear on right-wing talk radio that you can't hold an industry responsible when something they make is used criminally."

But a precedent has been established that does, indeed, hold companies liable for their products when they criminally contribute to death or injury; witness the tobacco settlements, successful suits against liquor and drug companies and asbestos manufacturers. Again, none of the products made by those industries are deadly by design, only by accident. That distinction continues to exclusively favor the firearms industry.

"What has to happen to get back to accountability by the gun industry is people have to understand that when someone is killed by a gun, someone needs to determine whether there was negligence along the way, from the manufacture of the gun to the sale of it. When there's negligence, then the surviving families of victims need to be compensated for the loss, and whoever was negligent—the gunmaker or the seller—needs to be punished in court. That's not what the Far Right calls frivolous lawsuits. It's accountability."

Part of the accountability Sarah Brady wants to see involves mandated safe storage of dangerous weapons, particularly at the retail level. There have been cases, some of which were pending in the courts at the time the Immunity Bill was passed, where guns were stolen from unlocked displays, only later to figure in shooting deaths. One such case was that of the D.C. snipers, two men, one a teenager, who went on a rampage killing people randomly on freeways and at filling stations. Before the carnage ended, the populace of the greater Washington area suffered from the mass fear of potentially being shot by a sniper. In that case, one of the perpetrators was able to simply walk off from a retailer with a deadly long gun called the Bushmaster.

"Look at the drug industry," said Sarah. "They're required by law to keep drugs that *could* be dangerous under lock and key. Why shouldn't people who sell guns, which *are* dangerous, be required to keep them safely locked away?"

Again, the point arises that without accountability for gun manufacturers and sellers thanks to the Immunity Bill, carelessness and negligence is left up to individual conscience rather than legal mandate. Will makers and sellers of deadly firearms go out of their way to ensure adequate safe storage when they are not required to?

To answer the question with yet another question, Would the tobacco, asbestos, and automotive industries have taken corrective steps to stop injury and loss of life had they not been required to be legally accountable? Would Vioxx have been pulled off the market by its manufacturer on its own if the Federal Drug Administration had not ordered the removal? Would Ford have stopped making the Pinto on its own after a number of fatal fires caused by a dangerous gas tank had they not been sued? Would the asbestos and tobacco industries have acknowledged the deadly nature of their products of their own volition or corporate consciences had there not been enormous court judgments against them?

And finally, are the above cases examples of what the Far Right calls "frivolous lawsuits"? Pose that question to anyone who has lost a loved one to lung cancer, asbestosis, dangerous prescription drugs, or deadly, flaming auto accidents.

I asked Sarah Brady what she thinks the future holds in terms of coming to grips with American gun violence. Her answer was candid, especially for one of the two namesakes of the organization in the forefront of the movement to stop gun violence.

"Look, we've hit rock bottom in the movement. We've lost momentum and suffered setbacks in Congress. It's looking bleak. But I'm confident the pendulum is about to swing back again."

She does not hesitate to place blame at the feet of the conservative movement that has succeeded in taking control of the White House and the Congress.

"The pendulum for the whole country is going to come back. You think we're going to be as conservative in the next elections [2006] as we were in the last? No, people are fed up with the ultra, ultraconservatives. And as long as we can focus on a positive agenda and show a need for it, people are going to start to see the problem.

"People are going to realize there's a connection

to terrorism in the issue. It's so easy for guns to get into the wrong hands, and they end up being exported abroad. We don't know how many. But we do know there are millions of guns made every year in this country. We're the largest manufacturer of weapons in the entire world. But look at Israel. They make a lot of guns—not as much as we do, but a lot. Do you think they let them get into the hands of terrorists?"

> "It's so easy for guns to get into the wrong hands, and they end up being exported abroad. We don't know how many. But we do know there are millions of guns made every year in this country. We're the largest manufacturer of weapons in the entire world."
>
> —Sarah Brady

Sarah believes the current acceptance of the gun violence epidemic is largely driven by the reality of politics and by the change in strategies and tactics of the NRA.

She echoes the assessment of the gun lobby held by Brady president Mike Barnes: "The history of the NRA was that through the 1960s it remained a sportsman's organization." But she feels that everything changed with the ensuing rise of conservatism. When Ronald Reagan was elected, the NRA was emboldened and confident they would see their political agenda met with a friendly White House.

"Luckily, Reagan didn't follow through and help them. But then crime was really getting bad. And you had all these fly-by-night gun manufacturers out in California [producing junk guns, cheap Saturday night specials]. They're not made anymore, thanks to laws that were passed to stop them. Even the company that put together the gun that Hinckley used to shoot Jim and President Reagan went out of business."

The California manufacturer in question was not allowed by law to make the kind of cheap handgun used by Hinckley, but they were allowed to import parts that could be assembled into such a gun.

"So the gun industry was falling on hard times after the seventies," Sarah said, connecting those hard times with the morphing of the NRA from a true sportsman's organization into what was to become arguably the most powerful and feared lobby in Washington. It was, she said, a perceived need to rescue an ailing gun industry, and the NRA chose to become the rescuer.

Another problem the gun industry has been facing is a shrinking market for its products as younger generations are not becoming interested in hunting and sport shooting to the extent their predecessors did. That perhaps explains the zeal with which the NRA is trying to find ways to protect its benefactors, the gun manufacturers, from further erosion. Granting immunity from legal accountability is one form of that protection.

Added to that is the increased cultivation of younger markets, with the hope of convincing teens, boys and girls alike, that hunting is an attractive activity to pursue with their families.

An article in *The New York Times* in September 2005 bore the headline "Girls and Boys, Meet Nature, Bring Your Gun." The story described the decline in hunters in America. The number of hunting licenses issued in the United States fell from 16.4 million in 1983 to 14.7 million in 2003, a decrease of 1.7 million, or more than 10 percent.

A spokesman for the National Shooting Sports Foundation, Steve Wagner, sees the loss of hunters as a diminished involvement by children, and he has launched aggressive efforts to reverse the trend with bills being introduced in Ohio, Pennsylvania, and Wisconsin to lower the age at which children can hunt or to loosen the requirements for a parent to accompany them while hunting.

Pro-gun groups such as the NRA and its allied organizations traditionally argue against new laws to solve gun violence, saying there are already too many gun laws on the books and all that is needed is to enforce them better. Yet Wagner's plan is to create new laws to get more and younger children into the field with guns.

Another advocate of recruiting more gun-wielding children into the field said, "Forty years from now our kids will be learning about this (hunting) as history. Hunters should be included as an extinct species because we're falling away so fast, we need to be protected."

Still another concerned hunter quoted in *The*

Times article, Kevin Hoyt, a hunting instructor, quit his job as a draftsman to dedicate himself to getting children interested in hunting. The father of five children under thirteen, he said he is committed to recruiting younger hunters. "My youngest child was with me when he was two months old and I shot a deer with a muzzle loader. He was in a backpack. I was stuck home baby-sitting and I felt like hunting," Hoyt said.

Hoyt also tries to speak at schools to recruit more children to hunting, but he reports that of 114 he has contacted, only ten have invited him to present his case.

"I hate to stereotype, but most teachers are liberal, tree-hugging, and they're not real sympathetic to the cause," he said.

Sarah Brady, of course, does not support attempts to get more and younger children hunting with guns. She also is not surprised at the decline in hunters, which she attributes to predictable changes in lifestyles and needs.

"The reason hunting was so big years and years ago was people lived way out in the country and needed to shoot possums and deer for dinner. It wasn't always for fun. But that's all changed. Now hunting is mostly for sport, not out of necessity. And that's fine. Target shooting is fine, too."

Our conversation turned to leadership, or lack of it, in reducing gun violence. When asked what presidents have been helpful on the gun issue, she replied,

"Well certainly, this Bush (George W.) hasn't. Clinton was wonderful. The only decent thing that "41" (George H. W. Bush) did was ban the importation of assault weapons, but he wouldn't do anything about domestic manufacture of them. He wouldn't sign the Brady Law. I think he gets a D."

Would she give Clinton a B? No, she said, he deserves an A. This from a woman who was an active Republican and has never been a Democrat.

Ronald Reagan? He too rates an A from Sarah. "He did well. He supported the assault weapons ban *and* the Brady Law. He also supported the banning of 'cop killer' bullets and, my all-time favorite, making sure there is enough metal in guns to be detected in security screenings. But when it came to a vote in Congress, a small handful of members, three or four maybe, voted against it. One of them was Dick Cheney."

Does that mean that Cheney and the gun lobby think there is nothing wrong with guns being manufactured that can go undetected through airport screening because of a lack of metal content? Sarah shrugged, as if to suggest one can draw one's own conclusion.

And, finally, the grade Sarah would give the current president, George W. Bush?

"Definitely an F," she said, without the slightest hesitation.

What would Sarah and Jim Brady like to see done to continue the fight against gun violence?

"Well, the Brady Bill was maybe the most effective

piece of legislation yet in keeping guns away from criminals," she said. "But that took seven years to happen. It was nonstop work at the state and the national level. So I would say to people in the movement, don't get discouraged. Maybe it will take three Congresses, but things can change. When we worked for the Brady Bill, we lobbied nonstop with the states we had to get with us.

"Illinois was a great example. Who would have thought Illinois would go for a bill like ours? But we stayed on them until they came around. Then we focused on states where we felt we could succeed. We looked at Florida. They're a good state on issues like this. So we worked hard with them and we got a three-day waiting period with a state initiative. We also got a safe-storage measure to protect children. New Jersey is a good state, too, with Senator Lautenberg [who sponsored an amendment to a gun safety bill that would have closed the gun show loophole nationally; the amendment failed, however, in the House]. We got a lot done in Maryland, with a ban of Saturday night specials, which, to no one's surprise, the gun lobby continues to oppose.

"So we were doing all these things in different states, which kept the gun lobby busy spending their resources to fight our efforts. And it made a big difference for us."

When I referred to the Bradys as heroes in the cause to stop gun violence, Sarah shrugged it off immediately, saying she and Jim simply decided to turn the tragedy that changed their lives so dramatically into a positive effort.

Jim will never walk again, yet he manages to travel the country in a specially equipped van that accommodates the wheelchair he is confined to. When he came to Denver to support the effort to close the gun show loophole in Colorado, he wheeled into a hotel ballroom, grinning broadly, with his familiar thumbs-up gesture. He delivered his remarks to an appreciative audience that seemed not to notice at all that his speech was slowed by the wound to his brain inflicted during the assassination attempt on his boss, Ronald Reagan. As grave as his wound was, the Bradys do not like to think of themselves as victims.

"Sure," said Sarah, "Jim was a victim of gun violence. But we don't like to dwell on that. You have to move on, to accept what you've got in life."

As for Sarah, she continues in her role as chair of the group that bears her and Jim's name. She has survived major illness and surgery, yet she persists in her energetic quest to bring what she sees as sanity to a national problem that continues to exact its toll on public health and safety in America.

If not herself and Jim, who does Sarah view as heroes in the cause?

"Always Ted Kennedy. He's never stopped being there for us. Senators Feinstein and Boxer of California, definitely. Congresswoman McCarthy of New York [who lost her husband in the Long Island

Railroad massacre]. Illinois has had some good ones, like the current young Senator Barack Obama. And years ago, there was George Ryan, who, as a Republican lieutenant governor back in the eighties, got an assault weapons ban passed, then went on to be governor of Illinois. And don't forget Senator Dick Durbin, also of Illinois, another strong supporter, along with Ohio's Governor Voinovich. When Howard Metzenbaum was in the Senate, he was one of the best on the issue, too."

Who are the antiheroes?

"That's easy," laughed Sarah. "All the others we didn't mention."

Who in particular?

"Oh, you've got Larry Craig, senator from Idaho, who votes consistently with the NRA, Orrin Hatch of Utah, Tom Delay, House majority leader [until he stepped down after being indicted on campaign funding violations]—he's the worst. Republicans in the South anymore, and most of the Democrats there, too, are not much help."

Not one to mince words, Sarah said, "Somebody who's really awful, just the worst, is Bill Frist (Senate majority leader). He's a doctor, a surgeon. More than anybody, he ought to know and understand this issue. It's just unforgivable.

"When we lobby," Sarah continued, "I tend to group reluctant members of Congress into two categories: the cowardly lions and the ones without a brain. You know, like in *The Wizard of Oz*. The cowardly lions are the ones who might not be opposed to what we're trying to do, but they're terrified of what the NRA would do to them if they support us. So we try to reassure them that we'll be there to help them if they're targeted by the gun lobby."

But the offer of support does not often work when a senator or representative is targeted by the NRA, given its history of driving moderates out of office in retaliation for supporting gun-violence reduction efforts.

"The ones without a brain, well they pose a different problem. We try to educate them on the problem and what the solutions are. But it can be a real uphill battle, even when the facts are staring them in the face. We'll never stop trying. Never."

> "I tend to group reluctant members of Congress into two categories: the cowardly lions and the ones without a brain. … The cowardly lions are the ones who might not be opposed to what we're trying to do, but they're terrified of what the NRA would do to them if they support us. … The ones without a brain, well they pose a different problem. We try to educate them on the problem and what the solutions are."
>
> —Sarah Brady

Chapter 4
The Right to Bear Hate?

I would never paint all opponents of gun controls with a broad brush of extremism or fanaticism. Yet there are some groups and individuals that have latched on to the gun rights movement to advance very different, sometimes troubling agendas, even white supremacy. Most defenders of Second Amendment rights thankfully have nothing to do with such abhorrent notions as racism.

That said, however, there is an alarming thread of exploitation of the fears of some gun owners that do their well-intentioned efforts great harm.

A visit to the Internet is all that is needed to witness that exploitation. When I typed in "Second Amendment Rights," one of the first Web sites that came up was a particularly virulent one that bills itself as a source for anyone interested in the right of "ordinary people" to keep and bear arms. Yet a visitor to the site need only scroll midway down the first page to see the true intent of the site.

The site is not nearly so much about gun rights as it is about crimes committed against innocent white children as the direct result of school integration in America's cities. A photograph of a badly scarred teenage girl is posted as proof of the dangers Caucasian children face in inner-city schools.

But the child is not, in fact, American. She is purportedly an English schoolgirl who was allegedly attacked by African knife-wielding immigrants when she came to the defense of another white child who was allegedly being bullied. As a result of the incident, the child needed stitches to close her wounds and would also require plastic surgery.

Whether the story is accurate or not, there is no explanation of what the incident has to do with dangers to American schoolchildren, other than the inference that it could easily have happened in a U.S. inner-city school. The reason for such danger existing in this country, according to the site? Racial integration that has been forced upon our schools to achieve racial and ethnic diversity. Further, any benefits of such diversity are denounced as "myth." The only genuine result of integration, the site continues, is the threat of violence committed on innocent white children by African Americans, who are responsible for wholesale crimes against Caucasians.

As preposterous as this so-called reporting is, it remains on the Internet, unchallenged, as a convoluted case for resisting efforts to reduce gun violence in America. In one outlandish non sequitur after another, the Web site defends the Second Amendment by citing everything from the need for racial consciousness to criticism of white Americans' guilt over slavery.

It would be comforting if that particular Web site could be dismissed as an anomaly, one that reflects views that rarely, if ever, appear in the gun rights versus gun-violence control debate. But, although the hatred spewed in the site's material is an extreme case, there are many others that continue to surface.

Consider the gun show near Dallas, Texas, a legally conducted sales event where, in addition to the usual array of weapons of all sizes, shapes, and power, a shocking display of racism was found in plain view on a display table, a message that had nothing to do with the sale of firearms. A stack of bumper stickers offered for sale bore a cartoon of a group of armed men in white hoods and sheets chasing after a frightened African American man. The caption on the bumper sticker read "The real boys in the Hoods."

Whether or not the bumper sticker was one rare and isolated incident, wherever gun regulation is advocated, passions often reach the point of inflammatory, even hateful invective.

In 2000, when SAFE Colorado campaigned for the initiative to close the gun show loophole, intolerance continually raised its head as part of the more extreme opposition to the measure. Even physical threats marred what was intended to be a reasonable debate between those favoring and those opposing background checks on all weapons sales.

Harassment became a matter of course during the months leading up to election day. As co-president of SAFE, I received much of it. A constant barrage of phone calls and anonymous messages accused me of everything from being a traitor and a Communist to single-handedly destroying the Constitution. Or worse. I, too, was warned that if I continued my work in behalf of the initiative that some vague, dire consequence would be visited on me.

Tom Mauser, father of Daniel Mauser, one of the thirteen victims in the Columbine massacre, was the most visible spokesman for the gun show initiative. In spite of the terrible grief he and his family bore after Daniel's death, he was a constant target of abuse and intimidation—anonymous, of course—by fringe opponents of firearms regulation.

One phone message in particular, left at the offices of SAFE, remains seared in the memory of Tom and all of us in the organization. It was the menacing voice of an angered man: "Mauser, I'd rather see a pile of dead kids than a pile of my guns taken away."

Another, even more troubling message: "I don't feel sorry for you, Mauser. You're just dancing on your dead kid's grave."

Most distressing of all for me personally was an incident that happened just two weeks prior to election day in Colorado Springs, a city known for its conservative politics, religious evangelism, a large retired-military community—and strong feelings about gun ownership.

I had been invited to present the case for closing the gun show loophole at a forum called the Citizens Project. I did not expect to be welcomed with open arms, as members of a gun advocacy group Pikes Peak Firearms Coalition (PPFC) demonstrated outside the entrance to the forum venue and filled about half of the auditorium seats. It was a stacked house, and I knew it.

When I was called on to present the SAFE Colorado position in favor of the initiative, I was greeted by heckling and obscene gestures from PPFC members. I did my best to state my case, which was made difficult by the distracting hostility of opponents in the audience. One man in the third row was particularly aggressive, sneering, shaking his head, and repeatedly flashing me his upright middle finger. I finally stopped my remarks and asked the angry man if he would be kind enough to put down his finger and allow me to finish my presentation uninterrupted.

At the end of the program, I started out of the hall. As I approached the exit, a large young man with a menacing sneer on his face stepped out of the shadows and confronted me.

"Are you Grossman?" he snarled.

"Yes, I am," I answered.

"You're a Jew?"

Trying to keep as much composure as anyone can in such a situation, I asked him, "What difference does my religion make?"

"You *are* a Jew, aren't you?" he demanded.

"Yes, I am," I answered, feeling everything within me recoil. "Are you an anti-Semite?"

"Yes, I am," he said unabashedly, raising his voice. "I hate you and I hate all Jews. The gun control movement is just a bunch of liberal Jews like you."

Of course, I realized it would do no good to remind him that Sarah and Jim Brady were neither liberals nor Jews. Or that the co-chairs of SAFE Colorado, former governors Richard Lamm and John Love, were Christians. Or that strong leadership and support for gun regulation came from the Council of Churches. Or, in fact, that a Wisconsin-based organization called Jews for the Preservation of Firearms Ownership describes itself as "America's most aggressive defender of firearms ownership" and uses the Torah to justify its case against gun controls. But that would have been an attempt at reason, which clearly was of no interest to the agitated man.

I stepped closer to him, glaring into his hate-filled eyes, and, in a voice I fought to keep lowered, said, "You are a fool, and I have nothing more to say to you," and turned away from him, stunned by his prejudice.

What is it about the gun debate that draws people with the kind of hatred that lives in the heart of that man in Colorado Springs, that prompts white supremacists to connect their racial paranoia to defense of the Second Amendment, that would drive someone to applaud the violent death of an innocent child to his grieving father?

One answer is, of course, an obvious one: these are merely isolated cases and do not reflect the views of the majority of responsible opponents of gun laws. Still, threats, intimidation, and racial and ethnic slurs continue to surface in the contentious debate over firearms.

Even more troubling are those occasions when the racist thread appears in the rhetoric of the most venerable of all pro-gun groups, the National Rifle Association.

The Violence Policy Center, a Washington non-profit foundation that conducts research on violence in America, has posted some alarming quotes from NRA spokespeople on its Web site. One is a statement attributed to Wayne LaPierre, NRA executive vice president, in an article he wrote for the magazine *American Rifleman*: "There are many politicians willing to sacrifice the Second Amendment as the first step in the homogenization of American culture." LaPierre subsequently denied that his remark had racial overtones when questioned by CBS News on *Face the Nation* and claimed that the NRA "has a proud relationship with the African American community" (the familiar "some-of-my-best-friends" defense). If "homogenization of American culture" does not contain racial overtones, what does?

Then there are the controversial remarks made in 1997 by Charlton Heston, a year before becoming the NRA's president, to the Free Congress Foundation. In his speech, Heston called on his audience to "draw your sword and fight." And who were the enemies to be fought? They included "blacks who raise a militant fist with one hand while they seek preference with the other." He continued to egg on listeners with the admonishment "Mainstream America is counting on you."

Isolated cases? The list published by the Violence Policy Center continues, including remarks made by an NRA board member of long standing, Jeff Cooper, who is also a columnist for the magazine *Guns & Ammo.* In one of his columns, he said, "No more than five to ten people in a hundred who die by gunfire in Los Angeles are any loss to society. These people fight small wars amongst themselves. It would seem a valid social service to keep them well-supplied with ammunition." This from a man who also has described people of Japanese ancestry as "Nips" and, according to the Violence Policy Center, once suggested calling black South Africans from the Gauteng Province "Oran-gautengs."

And this, according to the VPC's site, came from a research coordinator of the "mainstream" NRA, Paul Blackman: "Studies of homicide victims—especially the increasing number of younger ones—suggest they are frequently criminals themselves and/or drug addicts or users. It is quite possible that their deaths, in terms of economic consequences to society, are net gains."

No extrapolation is required to mine the meaning behind such words, which is abundantly clear in the message that when young inner-city men who are suspected—not necessarily convicted—of crimes such as drug dealing or usage are killed by guns, it's a good thing, a "net gain" for society.

In the 2004 presidential and congressional elections, which were clear victories across the board for conservative republicanism, former Democratic presidential candidate Howard Dean may have been the first to coin the phrase "God, Gays, and Guns" when describing the mood in the South, where George W. Bush gained enough of an edge to win reelection to the presidency that year.

Although many would argue that Dean went over the top in his characterization of southern voters, there is a clear link between people who are passionate about denying women the right to make reproductive choices and homosexuals the right to live in marital harmony while, equally passionately, defending the right of virtually anyone to own and use firearms.

When Charlton Heston famously held a rifle above his head and challenged critics to pry it "from my dead, cold hands," was he not saying that he and his followers would fight to the death for their gun rights? Is that passion not similar to the spewing of venom at gays and lesbians, calling them abominations and sinners, or worse? And when extremists opposed to abortion call for the death of doctors who perform the procedure, are they not acting out of the same kind of passion as Heston tries to ignite? Do people who ask us to choose life have the right to call for the death of those with whom they disagree? What of the religious fanatics who appear at funerals of gays carrying signs that proclaim "God hates fags," as they did at the memorial service for Matthew Shepard, the young gay man brutally murdered in Wyoming?

Michael Moore, producer and director of the documentary *Bowling for Columbine*, was reviled by gun rights advocates for his treatise on gun violence in America. During the 2004 presidential campaign, he also attacked the right wing of the Republican Party for turning patriotism into "hate-triotism," which earned him still more venom from the Right.

I personally believe that Howard Dean made a valid observation about the Right's linkage of God, gays, and guns in the heated political debate of the 2004 elections. It became apparent in that turbulent electoral year that there was much to be gained by conservatives playing to the fears of middle-class Americans. Thus, we heard from those who decry some godless movement afoot that would force all women to have abortions, that would turn heterosexuals into homosexuals, and that would send black helicopters swooping down to take away everyone's guns. This does nothing to serve the avowed purpose of protecting conservatives' constitutional rights, or anyone else's. Never mind that a gun, especially one illegally obtained, can so easily become the catalyst for the commission of the most ungodly of acts, in violation of everything sacred in all religions.

On one night in Denver, Halloween of 2005, three young men were shot to death in separate incidents within a four-hour span. In each case, drinking had been involved. Denver's chief of detectives urged parents to counsel their children about the deadly mix of guns and alcohol. But how likely are young people to heed such warnings when their elders insist on a heavily armed society with easy access to guns, even by those too young by law to own them, and when any attempt to restrict such access is viewed as a subversive, even ungodly, plot?

> "Young people believe they need to carry guns when they go out to have fun. They believe muzzle flash constitutes conflict resolution."
> —*Denver Post* columnist Jim Spencer

Commenting on that particular night of bloodshed, *Denver Post* columnist Jim Spencer said, "In an hour last weekend, seven young people in their late teens and early 20s were shot at two different Halloween parties in Denver. Three of those seven died."

Spencer said, "Americans so love their guns that Congress just voted to protect firearms manufacturers from lawsuits stemming from murders and maimings. In Virginia's governor's race, the Republican candidate runs on a platform that many think will become the next gun-lobby battle cry: allow people to carry loaded, concealed weapons in bars."

The column concludes, "Young people believe they need to carry guns when they go out to have fun. They believe muzzle flash constitutes conflict resolution.

"Congratulations to the gun nuts. They're winning the culture war.

"Now, if only we could interest them in picking up the bodies."

Chapter 5
Guns and Terrorism

All too often, a gun is both an instrument and a symbol of rage and hatred.

In rallies of protest throughout the Middle East, not only by militants such as Hamas but by Fatah and other more moderate factions, guns are waved and fired into the air.

More frightening, witness virtually every propaganda image of an American-hating jihadist parading an innocent hostage in front of TV cameras. What is always held in the hands of the terrorist? A gun. Why? Because it sends a message of power over the powerless, intended to instill fear, to force capitulation, to demean our nation and its people. It says, "Do as I say, or I will kill" or even, "I will kill even after you do as I say, because I have the power to destroy you."

That is not what the right to bear arms is about, by any wild stretch of the most perverse imagination. With the advent of terrorism, the new world war that has been predicted for years and in which we are now engaged, there is more need for vigilance than ever before in our history. And the

> "America's war on terror is the first in our history where we have fully collaborated in our enemy arming himself."
> —Former senator Gary Hart

question that must be asked is why we have not heeded the warnings that come from those who truly understand the risks we face.

Former senator Gary Hart in his foreword to this book warns that America's war on terror is the first in our history where we have fully collaborated in our enemy arming himself. He also cites a statement by a former senior Bureau of Alcohol, Tobacco, Firearms and Explosives official that describes the United States as "the candy store for guns in the world" and "absolutely" the best place for terrorists to buy weapons.

The message is as clear as it is frightening. The problem of guns getting into the wrong hands has gone beyond the already deadly trafficking to domestic criminals; it now involves easy access to American weapons to those whose aim is to destroy us. How can we pursue an aggressive war on terror when we have a gun distribution system that can facilitate it?

Another warning has been repeatedly sounded by Richard A. Clarke, former national coordinator for security and counterterrorism for Presidents Bill Clinton and George W. Bush and author of *Against All Enemies: Inside America's War on Terror.*

Clarke wrote a sobering essay in *Atlantic Monthly* in which he projected into the future to the tenth anniversary of 9/11. He created scenarios for each of the years following the attack on the World Trade Center in New York, a series of orchestrated terrorist attacks resulting in wholesale bloodshed and the eventual breakdown of national security and the very institutions that drive the nation, including the economy, in hopes of creating utter chaos and fear.

One particular scenario focused on the role that would be played by easily obtained firearms. In Clarke's fictional projection, terrorists choose a Sunday during the busy Christmas shopping season in some of the nation's largest malls in Minnesota, Texas, California, and Virginia.

The weapons used would be, in addition to dynamite, TEC-9 submachine guns and street-sweeper 12-gauge shotguns, with which shoppers would systematically be slaughtered, unable to escape the chaos.

"It had not been hard for the terrorists to buy all their guns legally in six different states across the Midwest," wrote Clarke. "A year earlier Congress had failed to reauthorize the assault-weapons ban." (The ban did actually lapse in 2005, but, if extended, it would have barred the sale of the guns to be used by the terrorists.)

Clarke went on to cite efforts by Attorney General John Ashcroft to have the FBI destroy records of weapons sales and background checks the day after the sale was made. Essentially this would make it impossible to track down a terrorist listed on a watch list who had amassed a cache of weapons at gun shows in order to carry out the kinds of attacks described in the scenario.

Yet Congress has continued to refuse to reinstate the weapons ban, which must surely encourage those bent on acquiring deadly weapons to carry out their agendas against the populace.

A report compiled by the Brady Center to Prevent Gun Violence states, "The gun is part of the essential tool kit of domestic and foreign terrorists alike. Guns are used to commit terrorist acts, and guns are used by terrorists to resist law enforcement efforts at apprehension and arrest."

The report also echoes concerns of federal and local law enforcement, calling the United States the "Great Gun Bazaar." A *Chicago Tribune* report tells of the discovery of a manual titled "How Can I Train Myself for Jihad" in the rubble of a radical Islamic terrorist group's building in Kabul. The manual points to the United States for its easy availability of firearms and advises Al Qaeda members living here to "obtain an assault weapon legally, preferably AK-47 or variations."

The patchwork of loosely regulated gun shows across the country has become a ready source for supplying the weapons terrorists are advised to accumulate. As if the dangers of domestic criminal use of guns passing through gun show loopholes has not been a serious enough threat, the international terrorist movement has taken things to a new level. And still, the gun lobby works relentlessly to keep the loopholes open, to fight congressional reinstatement of the ban on deadly assault weapons, and to resist federal record keeping on gun sales that would provide law enforcement with paper trails that could lead to apprehension of gun law violators. The result is a clandestine free-trade zone for the flow of weapons into the hands of terrorists, both domestic and foreign.

> The patchwork of loosely regulated gun shows across the country has become a ready source for supplying the weapons terrorists are advised to accumulate.

Corrupt gun dealers, the Brady report states, are allowed to funnel guns to terrorists because of what it calls "irresponsibility of the gun industry" as well as limits placed on record keeping of gun sales, which are the result of constant pressure by the gun lobby. Terrorists can buy assault weapons and high-capacity military magazines because of loopholes in federal laws and, more recently, because of the refusal of Congress to renew the assault weapons ban. Even the mails can be used by would-be terrorists to acquire untraceable assault weapons; gun kits that are offered through a federal loophole can easily be assembled into deadly automatic weapons.

All of which adds up to a genuine threat to the security of this nation, while resistance to any and all efforts to stop this dangerous activity continues in the name of the Second Amendment.

Given the above, here is yet another scenario that could happen at any time in almost any state in the nation:

A terrorist enters the country illegally into Texas, let's say, where there are no current laws to close the gun show loophole. He attends a weekend gun show, where any seller who is not a federally licensed dealer can sell guns without requiring background checks. In most states, even licensed dealers can conduct "no questions asked" sales by claiming to be offering for sale "personal collections." So, the terrorist sees a collection of semiautomatic weapons that can easily be modified with kits sold separately into fully automatic, and illegal, guns. Not only is the buyer not required to prove who he is or submit to a criminal background check, but the seller is not limited to how many guns he can sell to a single purchaser. What if the private seller says he has a hundred of the guns out in his truck? Can the terrorist buy them? Yes, very easily, in fact, in the anything-goes atmosphere of a gun show where the loophole exists.

Since most states have not closed the gun show

loophole, a logical question would be, Why hasn't Congress done so with federal legislation? It has been tried, and it has failed, with the closest attempt in 1999 when Senator Frank Lautenberg of New Jersey sponsored an amendment to require criminal background checks at all gun shows, whether sellers are licensed dealers or private sellers. The bill, which would have created uniformity of safeguards throughout the nation, resulted in a fifty-fifty tie vote, and the tie was broken by then–vice president Al Gore for the narrowest passage. But then the amendment died in the House of Representatives, where the gun lobby prevailed once more, and to this day there is still no federal requirement of universal background checks.

> The ATF estimates that there are more than 4,000 gun shows held annually in every region of the country. Most of those are not subjected to mandatory background checks from either licensed or unlicensed dealers.

There is a troubling irony in this situation: the government has created needed and stringent safeguards at every airport in the nation to detect and confiscate anything from boarding passengers that could pose a threat to air safety; even a cigarette lighter can be detected and taken. Yet that same federal government does not try to stop the illegal sale of deadly automatic weapons at gun shows to anyone with the money to buy them, even to buyers who might be intent on committing acts of terror with them.

The ATF estimates that there are more than 4,000 gun shows held annually in every region of the country. Most of those are not subjected to mandatory background checks from either licensed or unlicensed dealers.

How real is the threat of weapons bought at gun shows making their way into illegal gun trafficking channels?

The Brady report states that on September 10, 2001—the day before the terrorist attacks on the World Trade Center and the Pentagon—a man named Ali Boumelhem was convicted on weapons violations charges, as well as conspiracy to ship weapons to Hezbollah, the terrorist organization operating out of Lebanon. He and his brother Mohamed had bought a virtual arsenal of shotguns, assault weapon parts, and hundreds of rounds of ammunition at Michigan gun shows, according to press reports.

The Boumelhem brothers were arrested the previous November as they tried to leave the United States for Lebanon. Federal agents had observed Ali traveling to gun shows to buy weapons parts and ammunition for shipment overseas. Hezbollah, to which the weapons were believed to be shipped, was suspected of involvement in a number of anti–U.S. terrorist attacks, including the bombing of the Marine barracks in Beirut in 1983, an attack that killed 241 people. According to the State Department,

elements of the group were responsible for the kid-
napping and detention of U.S. and other Western
hostages in Lebanon.

In another case involving a suspected terrorist,
in 2001, Muhammed Navid Asrar, a Pakistani and an
illegal immigrant, had visited gun shows where he
bought several weapons, including a Ruger Mini-14
rifle, two pistols, and a hunting rifle. In Houston,
Texas, an FBI spokesman said that Asrar was investigated by ATF agents before the 9/11 attacks. He came
under scrutiny after asking employees of his convenience store to photograph tall buildings in Houston
and other cities. He was also investigated for possible
ties to Al Qaeda terrorists. And not once had he been
stopped or even questioned about his background or
citizenship while purchasing weapons at gun shows.
In October 2001, he pleaded guilty to immigration
violations and illegal possession of ammunition.

Another example of weapons flowing through
gun show loopholes to terrorists involved a member of
the Irish Republican Army, Connor Claxton, who was
reported as saying, "We don't have gun shows in Ireland,
and you see things here like you never imagined."

Shortly after arriving in the United States,
Claxton and three associates spent nearly $20,000 on
dozens of handguns, rifles, and high-powered
ammunition. They concealed the weapons in pack-
ages that they mailed back to Northern Ireland to be
used against the British government in terrorist attacks.
Law enforcement officers intercepted twenty-three

parcels headed for Northern Ireland and containing 122 guns and other weapons. In September 2000, Claxton, an acknowledged officer of the IRA, received a five-year federal sentence for shipping the guns to his native country. His colleagues each received shorter sentences for conspiring to help Claxton in his illegal shipments. The American gun dealer who sold more than 100 guns to Claxton's group cooperated with prosecutors, pleading guilty to conspiring to illegally export guns. He received only two years of probation.

Apparently, gun dealers who trade with criminals and terrorists through the gun show loophole are equal-opportunity traffickers. They even ply their trade with homegrown terrorists, like the white supremacist Benjamin Nathaniel Smith, who had failed in attempts to buy a weapon from a licensed dealer because a background check revealed that his former girlfriend had filed a protective order against him.

Not to be deterred by the law, Smith found Donald Fiessinger, who had accumulated more than seventy-two Saturday night specials, handguns preferred by criminals because they are easy to conceal and can be bought cheaply. Fiessinger reportedly bought the guns one at a time from a licensed dealer over a period of two years. With each purchase, he completed a sworn statement that he was buying a gun for his own personal use. He eventually offered his inventory in classified newspaper ads at nearly twice what he had paid at retail.

After buying a semiautomatic seven-shot concealable pistol from Fiessinger, Smith went on a shooting rampage in Illinois and Indiana, targeting religious and ethnic minorities. Before fatally shooting himself, he killed two people and injured nine others. He began in a Jewish neighborhood of Chicago, injuring six people at a synagogue. Then, in another neighborhood, he killed Ricky Byrdsong, an African American and former Northwestern University basketball coach, as Byrdsong walked with his children. On the following day, Smith shot and wounded an African American minister and an Asian American college student. And the day after those attacks, he fired his illegally purchased handgun into a throng of people at a Korean Methodist Church in Indiana, killing Won-Joon Yoon, a doctoral student of economics.

It was later learned that Smith had been a member of the World Church of the Creator, advocating supremacy over "mud people" with the stated purpose of "the survival, expansion, and advancement of the white race."

The gun dealer who illegally sold Fiessinger the cache of guns, one of which ended up in Smith's hands, after pleading guilty to knowingly violating state laws and receiving two years probation and a $1,600 fine, said, in a stunning understatement, "Maybe I could have stopped it. I could have saved some headaches."

As questions continue to rise concerning the ease with which terrorists are able to buy guns through gun show loopholes, the Bureau of Alcohol, Tobacco, Firearms and Explosives has warned that the problem lies as much with corrupt gun dealers as with the thousands of gun shows at which illegal transactions take place.

"Unlike narcotics or other contraband," says the ATF, "the underground gun market does not begin in clandestine factories or with illegal smuggling." All too often guns are diverted from licensed dealers into the illegal market.

The diversion of guns into the illegal market—and into hands of terrorists—reflects a failure of gun manufacturers to enforce effective business practices with their retail sellers. Critics of the gun industry point to what they perceive as a "look-the-other-way" attitude, even when manufacturers are aware of the dangerous illegal trafficking of their products.

> "(The) black market in firearms is not simply the result of stolen guns but is due to the seepage of guns into the illicit market from multiple thousands of unsupervised federal firearms licensees ... the industry's position has consistently been to take no independent action to insure responsible distribution practices."
> —Former Smith & Wesson executive Robert Hass

Someone who once worked within the gun industry, former Smith & Wesson executive Robert Hass, is quoted in the Brady report as saying that, in spite of the industry's knowledge that the "black market in firearms is not simply the result of stolen guns but is due to the seepage of guns into the illicit market from multiple thousands of unsupervised federal firearms licensees ... the industry's position has consistently been to take no independent action to insure responsible distribution practices."

As if corrupt gun dealers, along with a less-than-vigorous effort to stop their trafficking by manufacturers, were not a serious enough threat to national security, there are also the continuing and concerted efforts of the gun lobby to restrict enforcement powers of the ATF. While the National Rifle Association's mantra continues to call for simply better enforcement of existing gun laws rather than the enactment of new ones, the organization has a history of trying to weaken and discredit the ATF. The NRA also has the support of members of Congress such as U.S. Representative John Dingell, Democrat from Michigan and a former NRA board member, who called ATF agents "a jack-booted group of fascists" and "a danger to American society," as well as "a shame and a disgrace to our country."

How effective are the bullying tactics of the NRA and its vocal executive vice president Wayne LaPierre? In 1986, the powerful lobby led a successful effort to hamper the ATF's enforcement powers with the McClure-Volkmer Act. Under that act, ATF agents were limited to a single unannounced inspection of a licensed dealer in any twelve-month period;

prior to that new law, agents were allowed to inspect the inventory and records of a dealer "at all reasonable times."

Imagine any other public safety agency being told it can only investigate a business suspected of illegal and dangerous activity once a year. Also imagine the cover that could provide a dealer selling guns to the illegal market. What would there be to stop such a dealer from saying to a potential trafficker, "Don't worry, I've just had my one check of the year"? How effective could the DEA be in cracking drug rings or the FBI in seeking out terrorist cells if those agencies could only conduct inspections every twelve months?

Finally, adding to the dangers of gun show sales without background checks and the lack of responsible gun industry practices to curtail sales to traffickers is what Brady calls "mail-order terror." Again, because of loopholes in federal gun laws, a terrorist who does not want to be seen at a gun show or be identified by an illegal trafficker can resort to a flourishing mail-order business of selling kits with which deadly assault weapons can be easily assembled. As long as a manufacturer offers every part that goes into a firearm except the firing mechanism (which also carries the serial number of a gun), the sum of the parts sold as a kit do not constitute a firearm according to the loophole in the law. Thus, a buyer intent on obtaining a deadly assault weapon only needs to assemble the components, add something called a "flat" to a completed receiver, and he has a fully operable and legally obtained assault weapon, whether or not he has a criminal record or is illegally in the country and, therefore, not allowed to buy or own a gun.

> As long as a manufacturer offers every part that goes into a firearm except the firing mechanism (which also carries the serial number of a gun), the sum of the parts sold as a kit do not constitute a firearm according to the loophole in the law.

The availability of guns purchased as kits has been a problem for years. In 1994 in New York, a young Lebanese immigrant opened fire on a van of Jewish students as it crossed the Brooklyn Bridge, killing a teenage boy and wounding another. One of the pistols used by the gunman was an M-11/9 assault pistol, capable of firing eighteen shots in just seconds. The gun had no serial number that could have been traced. Why? Because it had been assembled from parts sold through the mail by a company in Tennessee. The owners of the company offered the $160 kit to anyone with a phone and a credit card, with no questions asked and no waiting period or background check to prevent sales to felons or juveniles.

When the seller of the kit was questioned about offering gun kits through the loophole in the law, his glib response was, "They're not guns. They're parts."

Kits to make the M11/9 assault pistol were advertised in shooting publications with headlines

such as "Yes! You can still build your own SEMIAU-
TOMATIC M11/9 firearm" and "No license
Required! Anyone can Purchase!"

When the origin of the gun used in the Brooklyn
Bridge attack was discovered, Representative Jerrold
Nadler, a Democrat from New York, introduced legislation in Congress to extend the federal ban on
firearms sales by mail to include key parts that can be
assembled into a gun. But to date, Congress has done
nothing to close this gaping loophole.

The Brady report concludes with a six-point plan
for preventing foreign and domestic terrorists from
obtaining deadly weapons. The following recommended
measures would not prevent law-abiding citizens from
lawfully buying, owning, and using firearms:

- Require complete criminal background
  checks for all gun sales, including all gun
  show sales.
- Retain federal background-check records,
  allow reasonable access to those records by
  law enforcement agencies, and repeal existing
  restrictions on gun-sale record keeping.
- Limit large-volume gun purchases to curb
  trafficking of guns to terrorists and criminals.
- Repeal provisions of the McClure-Volkmer
  Act that weaken the ATF's enforcement
  powers against corrupt gun dealers.
- Permanently reauthorize the assault
  weapons ban and strengthen it.

• Close the "parts kit" loophole.

It would seem that a program like the one offered by Brady would meet with little resistance, given its commonsense approach to keeping firearms out of illegal trafficking channels and equipping law enforcement agencies with the tools required to monitor and trace such trafficking.

Yet every recommendation continues to meet with opposition from the NRA and other gun-lobby organizations, and that opposition translates to a reluctance in Congress to take action that could substantially reduce the arming of terrorists by the American gun industry.

Those reluctant legislators and the White House would do well to heed the final caution of the Brady recommendations: "An assault weapon without a serial number is a terrorist's dream."

And an American nightmare.

Chapter 6
With Friends Like the NRA …

Henrik Ibsen's classic play *An Enemy of the People* tells the story of a doctor who has helped build a bathing complex in his hometown in Norway. When the doctor discovers that the baths are dangerously contaminated, he sounds the alert to the town's citizens. But his own brother and the mayor of the town pressure him to retract his findings to save the town from the financial losses the revelations would cause. The doctor refuses to recant and puts the safety of the citizens first. But he is demonized and painted as an enemy of the people, even though he is putting their safety first. His home is vandalized, and he and his daughter are fired from their jobs for speaking out. With his family's support, the doctor remains steadfast on his principles and says, "The strongest man is the man who stands alone."

That play serves as a fitting metaphor for the constant struggle of individuals who dedicate themselves to protecting society against the dangers of gun violence only to be demonized by the gun lobby. People like Tom Mauser continue to sound the warning, taking on the powerful NRA, willing to be the strongest man who stands alone, if necessary. His protests of the NRA's bullying tactics and resistance to gun law reform led to his arrest for trespassing when he demonstrated peaceably outside the lobby's national headquarters. But, like the man in the Ibsen play, he stands his ground, often alone, and tells his story with credibility acquired by the loss of his son.

There are others who, like Tom Mauser, know what it is like to have their lives irrevocably shattered by a bullet fired in anger, in psychotic desperation, or by tragic accident—in each case from a weapon that was either illegally obtained or carelessly left within reach of hands that should never hold a gun.

They are ordinary people who found themselves in extraordinary circumstances, such as a bus driver whose wife was randomly shot by a freeway sniper in Washington, D.C., or a man and a woman who both lost loved ones in senseless gun murders and were brought together by their tragedies and, now married to one another, dedicate their lives to ending gun violence. They are United States senators such as Ted Kennedy, who lost two brothers, one a president, the other a potential president, to assassination by gun, or Diane Feinstein, who lost close friends in a massacre in San Francisco's city hall. They, too, are champions of more-sensible laws to limit gun violence.

The gun lobby, with its inflammatory rhetoric, would have us believe that these advocates for an end to the killing are enemies of the people, when, in fact, they serve the people and public safety. How can anyone who appeals for safer streets, homes, schools, and public facilities be considered working against the people, an enemy?

Speaking of enemies, there is a list, compiled and published by the NRA and known as the "enemies list" by gun activists, that contains the names of organizations and individuals whose principle sin is opposing repeal of the lifesaving Brady Act and supporting reinstatement of the assault weapons ban that can help keep guns out of terrorists' hands.

Just a few of the so-called anti-gun organizations on the NRA's list are:

- AARP, which represents American seniors, many of whom are dedicated hunters but not adherents to the guns-for-anyone mentality.
- The AFL-CIO, representing workers of America, many of whom legitimately own and use guns for sporting purposes and, it can be assumed, are only opposed to guns in the hands of criminals and terrorists.
- The American Academy of Pediatrics. These are the physicians entrusted with the health and well-being of children. To whom are they enemies, other than intransigent lobbyists?
- The American Medical Association, the American Association for the Surgery of

Trauma (whose members man the nation's emergency rooms, where they try to put back together bodies torn apart by gunshots), the American Bar Association, the American Federation of Teachers, the American Psychological Association, the American Public Health Association, Common Cause, the National Association of Police Organizations, the National Coalition against Domestic Violence, the National Education Association, the National Parent-Teachers Association, Physicians for Social Responsibility, the Unitarian Universalist Association, the United States Catholic Conference, the United Methodist Church, the United Church of Christ, the Episcopal Church, the American Jewish Committee.

A list of enemies? It appears more like an honor roll of organizations that represent the very institutions that work for the better good, while doing no harm to any individual rights.

There is a similar list of individuals whose common crime appears to be lending their names and celebrity to gun violence reduction. Some of those names are:

Suzy Amis, Maya Angelou, Ed Asner, Alec Baldwin, Bob Barker, Kevin Bacon, Lauren Bacall, Candice Bergen, Tony Bennett, Jon

Bon Jovi, Peter Bogdanovich, Beau Bridges, Benjamin Bratt, Christie Brinkley, Dr. Joyce Brothers, James Brolin, Mel Brooks, Ellen Burstyn, Stockard Channing, George Clooney, Kevin Costner, Sean Connery, Sheryl Crow, Walter Cronkite, Matt Damon, Ellen DeGeneres, Michael Douglas, Gloria Estefan, Melissa Etheridge, Mike Farrell, Louis Gossett Jr., Mark Harmon, Dustin Hoffman, Hal Holbrook, Whitney Houston, Diane Keaton, Coretta Scott King, Lisa Kudrow, k. d. lang, Spike Lee, Madonna, Ed McMahon, Bette Midler, Paul Newman, Jack Nicholson, Leonard Nimoy, Sarah Jessica Parker, Michelle Pfeiffer, Dennis Quaid, Bonnie Raitt, Debbie Reynolds, Robert Redford, Anne Rice, Natasha Richardson, Julia Roberts, Martin Sheen, Britney Spears, Bruce Springsteen, Meryl Streep, Sharon Stone, Sting, Vinny Testaverde, Shania Twain, Sigourney Weaver, Oprah Winfrey, Vanessa Williams, and Catherine Zeta-Jones.

The list goes on, to almost laughable lengths, portraying many of America's most accomplished and socially conscious people and groups.

The list also raises an important question about the NRA: Who does that powerful lobby truly represent? If all those prominent Americans are the lobby's enemies, who are its friends?

It has been reported that fewer than 10 percent of American gun owners are actually members of, and therefore represented by, the NRA. It is an organization that was initially formed with the purpose of helping gun owners, particularly young ones, learn to shoot for sport safely. But over the years, the NRA evolved from a sportspersons' association to a political force to an arm of the Republican Party in its efforts to capture and keep the gun owners as part of its electoral base. And the efforts have been successful.

> Fewer than 10 percent of American gun owners are actually members of, and therefore represented by, the NRA.

What the NRA is in essence, then, is a powerful lobby group, perhaps the most powerful of all, which does not reflect the views of most Americans yet is able to block passage of laws designed to reduce gun violence and to silence members of Congress, even drive them out of office, for not supporting the industry's agenda.

Defenders of the gun lobby have pointed to the American Association of Retired People as an equally, or even more powerful force in the halls of Congress. But it simply is not true. Admittedly, AARP and the senior citizens it represents are powerful voices. They make their views heard with their votes to better meet the needs of aging, often poor Americans. Contrast that to the gun lobby's mission:

to block virtually every single piece of legislation designed to curb gun violence and to give its bene-factors, gun manufacturers, immunity from legal accountability for the deadly weapons they make and distribute. That immunity was officially granted in 2005 with landmark legislation that made gun companies the only industry in America to enjoy blanket immu-nity from prosecution and accountability, even when its members knowingly furnish illegal gun traffickers with weapons destined for criminals and terrorists.

Imagine the uproar in this country if the seniors' lobby succeeded in granting blanket immunity from accountability to elderly drivers who might kill or maim people with their cars, or if the medical pro-fessions got Congress to shield physicians and hospitals from accountability for death caused by malpractice, or to the food industry for poisoning people with contaminated products.

No, there is simply no valid comparison between the gun lobby and the lobbies that represent the rest of America's businesses, professions, and institu-tions. And bear in mind, the only industry that now enjoys immunity is the one that makes things designed to kill, not to help people, save lives, or edu-cate children.

If you were to ask an NRA member why the organization so vigorously opposes gun regulation in general, you likely would get an answer that refers to the "slippery slope." Those two buzzwords are a mantra for opponents of such measures as banning cop-killer bullets, Saturday night specials, and all-powerful assault weapons that can make criminals better armed than the police officers who confront them. Ban a bullet that can pierce inch-thick steel plate (or a police officer's protective vest), and, according to the slippery-slope argument, you begin a downward slide toward total disarmament of the entire population. Which is as logical as saying that if you prohibit children from smoking cigarettes or drinking alcohol, you risk a slide down a slope to banning alcohol and tobacco to all the population. Yet there is no shortage of defenders of the faith of guns for all and limits for none who will argue endlessly that controlling the availability of deadly weapons is a form of tyranny that must be stopped dead in its tracks down the imagined slope.

Buzzwords such as "tyranny," "slippery slope," and "gun-grabbers" seem to resonate with the more extreme elements of the gun-advocacy movement. They can inflame and propagandize an issue while they oversimplify it, obviating discourse and appealing to base emotion, playing to fears of something being taken away, even one's freedom. When a member of Congress offers a thoughtful case for banning deadly assault weapons, the response is usually not in kind, with a reasoned argument for their continued availability, but with the dire threat to liberty and an absolute right for everyone to own every sort of weapon. The argument gets more base than that, including tasteless assaults on the character of virtually anyone considered a part of the imagined tyranny.

In fact, one of the leading and more extreme gun-advocacy groups uses the very buzzword itself in its name: the Tyranny Response Team (TRT). This group appears at gatherings of groups like the Million Mom March, parading in Revolution-era costumes (which are as timely as their arguments) and banging drums slowly to lament the loss of freedom at the hands of tyrants (presumably mothers who want to protect children from gun massacres).

There are several TRT state Web sites on the Internet that post articles and quotes intended to support their resistance to gun regulation. One such posting bears the headline "Gun Control Works." Beneath the headline are four photos, identified as Hitler, Castro, Gaddafi, and Stalin. The message is as obvious as it is heavy handed: only despots would regulate guns.

> When a member of Congress offers a thoughtful case for banning deadly assault weapons, the response is usually not in kind, with a reasoned argument for their continued availability, but with the dire threat to liberty and an absolute right for everyone to own every sort of weapon.

But the anti-regulation propaganda goes from comically absurd to downright offensive, if not dangerous, in its vitriol aimed at proponents of gun sanity. A case in point: an article posted on the Maryland TRT chapter's site written by L. Neil Smith appears to advocate the jailing of any public office-holder who participates in legislation that would regulate firearms. It reads, in part:

> The Constitution, without qualification, states that the individual right to own and carry weapons will not be infringed. Title 18, U.S. Code, Sections 241 and 242, ordains as a crime the violation of anybody's civil rights. Part of the XIVth Amendment requires removal of any politician who defies the Constitution, barring him (or her) from public office in perpetuity. And, of course, betraying one's oath of office is perjury, which is a felony.

Never mind the enormity of that leap from the Second Amendment to the Fourteenth, but just observe the amazing logic offered from there:

> By attempting to ban semiautomatic weapons (or weapons of any sort), city authorities in Dayton, Ohio, and Rochester, New York, have broken all these laws. It's possible that conspiracy and racketeering statutes apply to their illicit activities, as well.

It continues:

Three things: they [the drafters of those laws, one would suppose] must repeal the offending legislation; they must resign from office immediately afterward; and they must promise, publicly and in writing, never to seek or hold public office again.

But here is where the comedy turns to the outrageous:

Meanwhile, we can offer them a few words of advice: don't listen to the torrent of lies spewed out by Sarah Brady and her fascist front-group. Don't let that pickle-faced harridan and her tent-revival meat-puppet [apparently referring to Sarah's husband, Jim] get you into more trouble ...

There you have it, the vilification of any lawmaker trying to reduce gun violence with responsible regulation, exceeded only by a viscous personal attack of the worst order on two dedicated human beings who turned the tragedy of gun violence into a life mission of preventing more destruction of innocent lives.

Perhaps most troubling of all is the question of whether the writer of that epistle owns or carries a firearm of any kind.

It is unfortunate that what could be a reasoned and productive debate over the issue of regulatory control of dangerous weapons too often turns into the sort of vitriol as exhibited in Mr. Smith's article, or worse. As is frequently the case in such debate, the extremists get much of the attention and those they oppose are labeled tyrants, fascists, or worse. Dialogue descends to the vernacular of the intolerant, and not only in the debate over guns. As mentioned earlier, two other flash point issues—God and gays—also descend into demonizing. Those who present legal arguments for keeping religion separated from government are called infidels and are condemned to damnation. Even the citizens of an entire city, Dover, Delaware, after voting out of office in 2005 school board members who had required public schools to teach religious doctrine in contradiction of evolution, were warned by evangelist Pat Robertson not to turn to God if natural disaster strikes them. Four years prior to that, Jerry Falwell blamed homosexuality and godlessness for the 9/11 terrorist attacks on the United States. When John Kerry questioned the war in Iraq, he was accused of being a traitor, even though he was a decorated war veteran who volunteered in the Navy in time of war while his most vocal critics served not at all. War hero and Georgia senator Max Cleland, confined to a wheelchair for life by his battle wounds from Vietnam, was driven out of office with similar smears from, among others, gun rights advocates who, ironically, questioned his patriotism.

What will it take to temper the heat and suspicion

that surface whenever gun laws are debated? From every indication, the NRA and its allied groups have no plans for toning down the rhetoric or easing the attacks on their perceived enemies, the friends of reasonable gun controls.

In October 2005, I interviewed Michael Barnes, past president of the Brady Campaign to Prevent Gun Violence. Long a thorn in the side of the NRA, he said of the powerful lobby, "The NRA has had a tragic impact. No special interest should have that power." Barnes, a former U.S. Marine and member of Congress, constantly tried to debate the leadership of the NRA during his six-year tenure with Brady, but the association's vice president, Wayne LaPierre, refused to engage in a dialogue about gun violence and accessibility of firearms.

One issue on which Barnes was particularly dogged in pursuit of LaPierre was the deadly Belgian-made assault pistol called the Five-Seven, which has also been named the "assault weapon that will fit in your pocket."

To prove just how deadly the Five-Seven is, a Brady staff member bought one and fired it at a police-style vest considered bulletproof. But a single shot fired by the weapon was captured on videotape easily piercing the vest, somber evidence of its firepower and of the advantage it would give to a criminal facing down a peace officer. Yet LaPierre dismissed the claim out of hand and continued to oppose banning the Five-Seven.

Barnes held a press conference in which he challenged LaPierre to put the Five-Seven, and a bulletproof vest, to the test. "If Wayne LaPierre is so sure of himself that the gun is not a threat to police, he should don a police vest and get a shooter of his choice to fire at it," said Barnes. LaPierre refused the opportunity to make his case, which, apparently, is that the right to be armed trumps the safety of cops wearing vests that cannot stop a legal bullet.

> "There's a direct correlation between strong gun laws and violence reduction. States with the weakest gun laws consistently record the most gun deaths, and, conversely, those states with the strongest gun laws have the lowest number of firearms deaths."
> —Michael Barnes, past president of the Brady Campaign to Prevent Gun Violence

Barnes also pointed out an inconsistency in LaPierre's constant response to proposals of additional gun regulation to reduce violence: there is no need for additional gun laws, since the ones already on the books do not stop the violence.

"That's just not true," said Barnes. "There's a direct correlation between strong gun laws and violence reduction. States with the weakest gun laws consistently record the most gun deaths, and, conversely, those states with the strongest gun laws have the lowest number of firearms deaths."

An example he pointed to is Alaska, the state with the highest rate of gun deaths in the nation. It is also a state with virtually no gun laws. Other states with some of the highest gun death rates in the country include Mississippi and Louisiana, which, again, have the lowest number of gun laws on the books. New Jersey, New York, Hawaii, and Massachusetts, according to Barnes, record the lowest per capita gun death rates in the country, along with the largest number of laws regulating guns.

Turning to political makeup of states, Barnes said, "The reddest states are the deadliest; the bluest are the safest when it comes to gun violence. You are six times more likely to be shot in a Republican western state than in Democratic New York."

Things are changing, though, in the states that have, in the past, been taken for granted by the gun lobby, particularly in the West. Colorado and Oregon have moved toward a more progressive posture by closing the gun show loophole. Montana, generally considered a safe Republican state where guns are a way of life and gun ownership is a GOP issue, elected a Democratic governor, Brian Schweitzer, in 2004, by a large margin. He is a hunter and gun owner but is also viewed as a progressive and populist.

> If there is a gun in your home, it is twenty-two times more likely to be used against family members than against intruders.

Responding to another claim by LaPierre that a home with guns in it is safer for its occupants than one without them, Barnes cited statistics showing that if there is a gun in your home, it is twenty-two times more likely to be used against family members than against intruders.

As vocal as Wayne LaPierre is, seeking every opportunity to present his case for more guns and fewer laws to control them, he shies from debating the issues with Michael Barnes. The offer has been made repeatedly but never accepted.

"The NRA doesn't like to talk specifically about guns. They always try to shift the argument to the Second Amendment. Their message of choice, carefully crafted for maximum resonance among their base, is about freedom, about individual rights. And we have to accept that it's a message that's very appealing to a lot of people," said Barnes.

"We win the debate when we talk about specifics, asking people simply, 'Do you want your next door neighbor to have an Uzi in his home? Do you want criminals to have easy access to deadly weapons? Those issues become more important to average Americans than notions of some vague conspiracy to trample individual rights."

Barnes paints a far more ominous picture of the NRA than one of an organization protecting individual freedoms or serving sportsmen and -women.

"It's all about money now," he said.

It's business, the business of serving and protecting rights, not of hunters and sporting shooters, but of the arms industry to keep making virtually every kind of weapon it chooses, with no risk of accountability for the havoc its products cause, thanks to the immunity law.

They have, in fact, become the criminals' lobby, the terrorists' lobby. They work to make it easier to obtain guns that can be used against law enforcement and society. Law-abiding sportspeople? The NRA doesn't advocate for them; they use them to achieve their goals.

Add to that the lobby's appeal to some sense of manhood and the fact that so many politicians are afraid to stand in opposition to the NRA, and you can see the dimensions of the problem. Senator Joe Tydings, back in 1968, saw those dimensions when he was voted out of office, with the help of an NRA smear campaign, for daring to advocate for gun controls.

Finally, Barnes said, "It's all politics now. The NRA has become an arm of the Republican Party with a mission to control the government of the United States."

Those thoughts are echoed by Brian Malte, outreach director for the Brady Campaign and an indefatigable champion of gun violence reduction at the state level.

"The problem with what the NRA puts out is that the press generally takes it and runs with it. Too often the attacks are taken as truthful and succeed. The NRA in effect got Senate Minority Leader Tom Daschle out of office and openly brags about it. They supported Mel Martinez for the Senate in Florida because of his pro-gun positions, and he won."

Apparently those are precisely the two formidable things the NRA can accomplish: victory for opponents of reasonable gun regulations and defeat for those who support them.

Apparently those are precisely the two formidable things the NRA can accomplish: victory for opponents of reasonable gun regulations and defeat for those who support them. But what they seem completely disinterested in accomplishing is enactment of laws that can reduce gun violence in America. New laws involving guns are wrong and should be avoided at all cost, they say. And they kept saying it right up until they managed to whip the U.S. Congress into doing what? Passing a new law involving guns, in the form of unprecedented protection for the industry they serve.

On the morning of my interview with Mike Barnes, I picked up the day's *Washington Post* and was greeted by yet another headline delivering the news of an overnight gun tragedy:

Gunman Opens Fire in Shopping Mall; Six Hurt, Three Taken Hostage (Associated Press, Tacoma, Washington, November 21, 2005)

A 20-year-old man opened fire with an AK-47 assault weapon, firing randomly and repeatedly at shoppers, critically wounding one and terrifying weekend shoppers. His weapon is the type that had been illegal under the assault weapon ban, which Congress allowed to lapse. But it remains illegal in the hands of a convicted felon, which the man was, with an extensive juvenile record, as well as being under a court order not to posses any weapons.

The story did not reveal where and how the shooter illegally got an assault weapon. And the gun lobby continues to oppose criminal background checks at gun shows, while sounding its familiar mantra: "More guns, less crime."

When someone like the mall shooter in Tacoma, who could not legally buy a gun because of a felony record, manages to get a weapon like the one he used, it is difficult to pin down the channel through which it was bought. One opportunity that gives criminals access to guns is the notorious "straw purchase." What it amounts to is someone who can legally buy a gun from a dealer by simply claiming it is for his own use while the real buyer, who cannot pass a background check, waits nearby or brazenly right next to the straw purchaser. It is not unlike an underage teen asking someone of legal age to buy liquor for him or her, waiting outside the store for the purchase. But the waiting buyer of an assault weapon can have a far more ominous intent in the straw purchase. Like a plan to kill people. An unlikely scenario? Guns

> One opportunity that gives criminals access to guns is the notorious "straw purchase." What it amounts to is someone who can legally buy a gun from a dealer by simply claiming it is for his own use while the real buyer, who cannot pass a background check, waits nearby or brazenly right next to the straw purchaser.

purchased for the underage shooters in the Columbine massacre were obtained by straw purchases. Someone was willing to break one law to enable two troubled youths to break a far greater law and commit wholesale murder as a result.

In its report "Smoking Guns," the Legal Action Project of the Brady Center described efforts to uncover flagrant gun-law violations through straw purchases. It cited an undercover sting operation conducted by Chicago police leading to the city filing a lawsuit against the gun industry. Pairs of covert officers visited gun stores to make straw purchases. According to the report, one officer would state clearly that he was a convicted felon or underage. In nearly every case, the dealers agreed to supply guns to someone who was obviously an unlawful buyer.

One dealer visited in the sting repeatedly broke the law and routinely allowed straw purchases, including a sale to an undercover officer who said he could not legally buy guns for himself because he had recently been jailed in another state. A clerk simply watched as the unlawful buyer chose a gun and handed the money to his friend to pay, then walked out the door with the weapons. In another case, the same dealer sold a gun to an undercover agent who said he had to throw away his 9mm pistol while running from police and he needed to "settle up" with an informant who had "ratted on him." In still another case that defies belief, the dealer sold guns to an officer who claimed he needed them to kill someone— someone who had previously shopped with him at the store. The clerk recommended a Tec-9 assault pistol capable for firing 100 rounds per load, saying, "This will take care of business."

The Chicago sting was featured on CBS's *60 Minutes*. Detroit police decided to try a similar sting to learn if the widespread publicity given to the straw-purchase problem on television would inhibit such dealings in their city. They clearly did not.

As in the Chicago operation, Detroit undercover officers made it clear that a buyer with a clean record was purchasing for a criminal or juvenile. Nine out of ten dealers visited eagerly made the illegal sales. In one case, a clerk told officers that "This is called a straw purchase," repeated twice that "It's highly illegal," and went ahead to sell the gun wanted by the illegal purchaser.

Other transactions in the sting included a licensed dealer selling to a purchaser for a juvenile at a gun show. The dealer said, "I could get in a lot of trouble for this ... I don't care. ... This question right here (on a required form) says 'Are you buying this gun for yourself?' Now all three of us know you're not, know what I'm saying?"

Another dealer completed the straw purchase transaction while mimicking the cries of parents grieving the loss of a child to gun violence, according to the Legal Action report. His imitation included, "You see them people down there (picketing at the city/county building) walking around bitchin' and runnin' their mouth, boo-hooing and 'Oh I'm so sorry I lost my son, and he was going to be this or the next Einstein or something, and he got killed and I just don't know what I'm going to do. ... '"

Compassionate conservatism? Apparently it's just good business in the eyes of gun dealers who choose to look the other way or wink at an obvious straw purchase. A particularly egregious case was in Texas, where one of the state's largest gun dealers, Carter's Country, allegedly directed its employees to encourage straw purchases in order to avoid losing sales. An employee there testified that customers sometimes disclosed they had felony records and, "We were directed on several occasions, find out if they've got somebody with them or can get somebody to come do the legal work to buy the gun, which to me is a straw purchase, illegal." The clerk raised the issue with management several times and claims to have been told, "Well, you don't worry about that." When she refused to make a straw sale on one occasion, management chastised her, she said, for turning away a $900 sale.

The gun industry has paid lip service to efforts to eliminate straw purchases by criminals, including support by one trade association, National Shooting Sports Foundation, of a program called "Don't Lie for the Other Guy." Still, the gun lobby at large continues to oppose the kind of legislation that would drastically reduce, if not eliminate, the deadly sales that continue to arm criminals and juveniles. The NRA continues its familiar rhetoric of "No new laws; just enforce the old ones" and its easily disputed but infrequently challenged hallmark slogan: "More guns, less crimes." But as crime continues to grow along with the numbers of guns in society, as loopholes continue to provide open doors for illicit gun trafficking, the NRA hyperbole tends to lose its relevance and credence.

Chapter 7
Blowing the Whistle on the Gun Industry

When abuse or misconduct abound within an industry or its paid fronts, the most compelling stories of the malfeasance frequently come from within, from people driven by conscience to take the risks to career and reputation so the true story can be told.

One such risk taker is Robert Ricker, a former NRA attorney, gun lobbyist, and trade association director.

In an interview for this book and in a Legal Action Project publication, "Smoking Guns; Exposing the Gun Industry's Complicity in the Illegal Gun Market," Bob Ricker revealed an alarming insider's story of gunmakers' and their lobbyists' take-no-prisoners tactics to obstruct legitimate efforts to reduce gun violence in America.

Ricker worked in the gun industry for nearly twenty years, representing interests of gun owners, manufacturers, distributors, and dealers. He joined the National Rifle Association in Washington as a lawyer in 1981 and later went to the West Coast, where he was a consultant to gun organizations, including the NRA and its affiliate, Gun Owners of California. He also represented the Citizens Committee for the Right to Keep and Bear Arms and the National Alliance of Stocking Gun Dealers. One of his accomplishments in that capacity was writing the first state statute granting legal immunity to the gun industry. The law, which exempted gunmakers from some product liability suits, was eventually repealed by the California legislature in 2002.

Ricker eventually returned to Washington, where he became an executive of the American Shooting Sports Council (ASSC), the largest and most powerful trade association that lobbies for the gun industry. The ASSC's membership roster included nearly all major gun manufacturers and distributors. His next move was to the position of assistant general counsel for the National Rifle Association, which was to become his last professional involvement with the firearms industry and its lobbyists.

It was in 2003 that Ricker reached the point where he could no longer remain silent about the gun industry's misconduct, and he dropped a large bombshell that shook the manufacturers and their lobbyists to the core. He issued a detailed declaration in support of lawsuits filed by twelve California cities and counties against the gun industry.

In his declaration, Ricker claimed that the industry has long known that massive quantities of guns are diverted regularly to the illegal black market through such avenues as "straw sales, large-volume sales to gun traffickers, and various other channels by corrupt dealers or distributors who go to great lengths to avoid detection by law enforcement authorities."

In spite of its knowledge of such dangers, Ricker continued, the industry refuses to take steps to stem the flow of guns to criminal elements. He said, "Leaders in the industry have long known that greater industry action to prevent illegal transactions is possible and would curb the supply of firearms to the illegal market."

Reading the Ricker declaration brings to mind images of chief executives of America's major tobacco companies standing before a Senate committee and, one by one, right hands raised, declaring under oath that nicotine in the products they make and sell has not been, to their knowledge, addictive—before internal memoranda very much to the contrary were uncovered.

> Ricker claimed that the industry has long known that massive quantities of guns are diverted regularly to the illegal black market through such avenues as "straw sales, large-volume sales to gun traffickers, and various other channels by corrupt dealers or distributors who go to great lengths to avoid detection by law enforcement authorities."

The gun industry is as notorious as the tobacco manufacturers for being in a constant state of denial when its profits are at stake. Never mind that the products both industries make and sell have been proved dangerous to public health time and time again; the stonewalling continues. The difference between the two industries is that one, tobacco, has been held financially accountable for the deaths caused by what it makes, while the other, gunmakers and sellers, have not and will not be in the future, thanks to the success of the NRA's lobbying efforts that gave them an unprecedented free pass.

Today Bob Ricker serves as a legal consultant to the Coalition to Stop Gun Violence, a Washington-based advocacy organization allied with the Brady Campaign, Million Mom March, and other groups with a mission to reduce gun violence in America. And he did so at no small personal cost. As soon as the NRA learned of his move to what they perceive as "the enemy side," the association resorted to the retaliatory tactics for which it is known, according to Ricker.

When he left the NRA to work with the Brady Campaign, Ricker said he quickly lost four of his major consulting clients. "It was so obvious. I was punished by the NRA, which put pressure on my clients when I advocated background checks in all gun purchases. They considered me too much of a liability for the shooting-interest clients whom I had planned to continue representing.

"The NRA's strategy is to win, and they will do everything and anything to make sure they do win, short of breaking the law."

Even though they will not break the law, the NRA seems very willing, if not dedicated, to the most egregious forms of retribution and intimidation, such as trying to drive a man out of business for opposing their goals, as they tried to do with Ricker.

Although his adversaries in the gun industry might characterize Ricker as a "gun grabber," or a total abolitionist of gun rights, the portrayal is far from accurate. In fact, he is a gun owner and a hunter. Like millions of other moderates on the issue, Ricker believes in the rights of Americans to own and use firearms, but also that the right should be denied to criminals and others who pose a danger to society.

> "I believe in the Second Amendment. I believe that it means I have a right to own a gun. But it's not absolute. There's a balance that has to be there."
>
> —Robert Ricker, former NRA attorney

"I believe in the Second Amendment. I believe that it means I have a right to own a gun. But it's not absolute. There's a balance that has to be there. It's like the First Amendment. I know it's a cliché, but it's true, that your right to free speech does not give you the right to shout 'fire' in a crowded theater. There have to be similar limits to gun rights. Even the NRA recognizes that the Second Amendment does not provide an absolute right to own a gun."

That said, however, Ricker also points out that the NRA still marginalizes everyone who raises the question of the limits of the Second Amendment. "If you support regulation of guns, you're a gun grabber. Which again, if the NRA is to be believed, makes the majority of the millions of owners of sporting and hunting guns who support reasonable regulation gun grabbers. And from whom do they wish to grab—themselves?"

A similar story of members of the gun industry speaking out about dangerous practices of distribution involved owners of a gun shop in North Carolina, Carole and the late Bill Bridgewater, who also were officers of the National Alliance of Stocking Gun Dealers. Carole Bridgewater, like Bill Ricker, went public with claims that manufacturers and distributors eagerly sell guns to any dealer with a federal firearms license, even though they know full well that most of the so-called dealers "are not real, legitimate, responsible businesses." She also claimed that while many licensees willfully ignore laws governing gun sales, manufacturers and distributors "not only tolerate these dealers but also actively feed them."

She went on to state that "It is well-known in the industry that ATF has issued federal firearms licenses

> "If you support regulation of guns, you're a gun grabber. Which again, if the NRA is to be believed, makes the majority of the millions of owners of sporting and hunting guns who support reasonable regulation gun grabbers. And from whom do they wish to grab—themselves?"
>
> —Robert Ricker, former NRA attorney

to felons, even some who used their prison address to obtain the license while still incarcerated … people have obtained federal firearms licenses in their dogs' names."

The result of such mis- and malfeasance by the industry, according to Bridgewater, is that the industry's "willingness to sell guns to anyone with a federal firearms license feeds the black market for guns," a problem that also "makes it extremely difficult for legitimate dealers who obey the rules to compete and survive."

The picture insider Bridgewater painted is a troubling one, not only of an industry that looks the other way when outrageous licensing abuses are tolerated but also of a system that actually punishes legitimate dealers who choose to obey all the rules, suffering business losses because of their unwillingness to follow the lead of their unscrupulous competitors.

It is easy to imagine incredibly dangerous scenarios created by the abuses mentioned by Carole Bridgewater. The cynicism and blatant disregard for the law that would prompt a prison inmate to obtain a license, using his jailhouse address, or applicants to actually use their dogs' names might appear to be low comedy but is in reality a deadly serious example of fatal flaws in the system. These are black market weapons of deadly destruction, not counterfeit Gucci handbags. Someone resorting to such tactics to get a license clearly has something to hide from authorities. Does it not follow that the manner in which they will sell their firearms, and the people to whom they will sell them, also need to be hidden? A terrorist with no identification, bent on killing perceived enemies on American soil, is obviously going to choose to do business with a "dealer" whose license bears the name Rover. And does it not also follow that a manufacturer, even a government agency, the ATF, are at best woefully lax or indifferent to the abuses and at worst complicit in them?

Still another member of the industry, Robert Lockett, a Kansas gun dealer and columnist for *Shooting Sports Retailer,* went public with a call for manufacturers and distributors to "wake up" and control their distribution systems, requiring dealers to "adhere to some strict guidelines."

In one of his columns, which was allegedly watered down by editors before publication, Lockett wrote, "I've been told innumerable times by various manufacturers that they 'have no control' over their channel of distribution. … IF YOU DO NOT KNOW WHERE AND HOW YOUR PRODUCTS ARE ULTIMATELY BEING SOLD—YOU SHOULD HAVE KNOWN OR ANTICIPATED THAT THEY WOULD BE ILLEGALLY SOLD AND SUBSEQUENTLY MISUSED. Let's get down and dirty. We manufacture, distribute, and retail items of deadly force."

In typical industry fashion, Lockett soon felt retaliation for daring to take manufacturers and distributors to task. Several distributors meted out economic punishment, refusing to continue selling their products to Lockett. Even the magazine that carried the column was punished by makers of Glock guns, which, Lockett claims, withdrew its advertising from the publication.

Lockett was not deterred by the industry's efforts to ignore or silence him. Although he did not succeed in changing manufacturers' policies, he continued his efforts for reform by adopting a set of strict guidelines for his own gun shop, which were intended to do the job the industry has not done. They include:

- Keeping a computerized record of the number of guns sold to any customer in a twelve-month period.
- Requiring salespeople to demonstrate safe functioning and handling of guns sold.
- Requiring purchasers to show an ability to safely use guns bought.
- Requiring buyers to disclose plans for safe storage of guns and for preventing unauthorized use.
- If a gun is sold with a safety lock, requiring salespeople to demonstrate effective use of the lock and the buyer to show an ability to do so.
- Requiring both salespersons and customers to complete forms attesting that all of the above policies have been followed.

The measures Lockett instituted in his gun shop

were entirely of his own volition, based on his frustration with the lack of such preventive safety measures. Of particular importance is the first of his policies, keeping track of the number of guns sold to individual buyers within a year, a way to create a paper trail of multiple purchases that can enter the gun-trafficking network, a measure that the NRA has always opposed and will continue to vigorously oppose in the future.

Chapter 8
Ordinary People in Extraordinary Circumstances

Jennifer Bishop and Bill Jenkins are married. They met and they fell in love, and realized they should be together because of what they had in common. It sounds like a typical story of two people finding one another in some happy circumstance. But, in fact, their relationship began neither typically nor happily. What they had in common was the utter and senseless tragedy of the violent death of loved ones by gunshot, the worst sort of serendipity.

They are two of the thousands of faces behind the terrible statistics of American gun violence. They are among the surviving loved ones who must find ways to live after those close to them die at the hands of murderers in a country that seems to take such deaths as just more faceless numbers every day of the year.

Jennifer was a schoolteacher and assistant principal living in the Chicago area before tragedy struck her family. Today she works as a victims' activist, serving as a field director for the Brady Campaign to Prevent Gun Violence. When asked what brought her to the gun violence movement, her answer comes matter-of-factly, as though she has repeated it countless times. It soon becomes apparent that what seems like detachment is an attempt to cover the deep pain that will never leave her, to ward off the tears that eventually come and cause her to stop speaking long enough to regain her composure, as was the case throughout our interview.

"My youngest sister, Nancy Bishop Langert," she began, spelling the last name, "and her husband, Richard Langert, and their unborn child were shot to death by a sixteen-year-old named David Biro on April 7, 1990. My sister was five months pregnant with their first child. So the courts tried it as a triple homicide.

"We were all out on a Saturday night, celebrating my father's birthday. It was Palm Sunday weekend, and Nancy was very excited about her pregnancy. She was ultracareful. She wouldn't eat chocolate or drink coffee or pop; she was very careful about caffeine during the pregnancy. Early in the evening, she said she was going home to bed. She was just so careful about protecting her unborn baby. She and Richard got home to the townhouse in Winnetka, Illinois, where they were staying while they were preparing to move into the first house they had purchased. Just a short distance from the townhouse was a $3 million mansion in which David Biro lived."

Jennifer had to stop here and remained silent for a short time, breathing deeply, waiting for the tears to pass, before continuing.

"One of the things we think drove him to choose

my sister and brother-in-law at random was simply the location. All he had to do was cross the street and then go through the grounds of the small Winnetka police station to the house. We really don't know why he chose to shoot them. But he seemed to be saying, 'Look what I can do right under everyone's nose, right in front of the police, and get away with it and then just walk back home.'"

Jennifer described David Biro as the youngest of three children, an outstanding high-school student with a near-perfect grade average. Her father knew the parents, whom she described as "very nice and very busy people," but also neglectful parents. "At age sixteen," she said, "this kid had far too much time on his hands, and far too little supervision."

As Jennifer described the setting for the murder, one of the wealthiest communities in Illinois, the story flew in the face of the profile of murderers with guns that are so often drawn by opponents of gun controls: poor urban kids, usually minorities, members of gangs, from broken and disadvantaged homes, prowling their ravished neighborhoods in search of drugs. When something like this murder takes place, the response is often, "We're so shocked; you just don't expect something that terrible to happen here." And the "here" means nice, clean, and very white suburbia, where people just don't shoot other people. Which was the shocked reaction repeated over and over in Colorado when two middle-class white boys went on their horrific rampage at Columbine High.

"Biro had actually been diagnosed as a dangerous sociopath because he had started committing a series of crimes in his sophomore year of high school," said Jennifer. "In addition to his straight As, he was a varsity track athlete. And he ran for student council president. He was definitely thought of as a brain, but he did bizarre things to get attention. He was amoral and alienated, sort of the Columbine profile. He did things just to break the rules, to show he was smart enough to get away with it."

Jennifer described a list of crimes, details of which were later discovered in his bedroom, crimes that he wanted to commit, which again recalled the behavior of the two Columbine killers in the lead-up to their rampage; they too had drawn up lists of things they planned to do, including committing mass murder.

"He would snipe at passing cars with a BB gun from his bedroom window, once shooting out a windshield in the process. He once even set a girl's sweater on fire at school. In this huge house, he had the whole third floor to himself, which he kept padlocked. Behind the locked door he had guns, he had robbery equipment, like glass cutters, which he practiced with in preparation for planned burglaries. He got handcuffs from a pawnshop and practiced using them too. He also had computers he had stolen from his high school in his locked room. And all the while, his parents knew nothing of what he had hidden up there and what things he did there. Which is why we eventually sued them."

It took an attempted poisoning by Biro—of his own parents, with chemicals that he stole from a school chemistry laboratory—for his family to finally do something about his behavior.

"His parents finally put him in a hospital," said Jennifer. "After two weeks, they were told, 'This kid's dangerous. You've to keep him here for a good long time.' But school was about to start, and his parents said, 'No, no, we're not going to keep him out of school. It's no problem, we'll keep an eye on him.' So they pulled him out of the hospital, and, six months later, my sister was dead."

Jennifer described how, after leaving the hospital, Biro conspired with a friend to get a FOID (firearm owner identification) card, which is required by the state of Illinois to purchase a firearm or any ammunition. He lied about his age, saying he was twenty-five (the minimum age for buying a gun was twenty-one at the time) and used his friend's date of birth and background records.

Biro's parents happened to intercept the forged card when it arrived in the mail and turned it over to an attorney who had defended their son in previous brushes with the law, including setting the girl's sweater on fire. By then, Biro had also put together an all black outfit, which he kept locked in his bedroom, an outfit that included a black knit cap, black leather gloves and boots, and a black trench coat.

"That outfit he assembled," said Jennifer, "was

nearly the same as the ones worn by the two student killers at Columbine—eight years before that massacre took place."

When the parents confronted their son about the card they had intercepted, Biro's response was to phone the lawyer and demand return of the FOID card, saying he could take it back if he had to, boasting of his burglary skills. Jennifer described a bizarre series of events that then followed, including the attorney retaining a security expert to check his office to make sure it was secure against a burglary. He also locked the FOID card away in a safe. But, incredibly enough, according to Jennifer, the attorney neglected to lock away a .357 Magnum handgun, along with six speed loaders, accessories that allow a shooter to quickly place six bullets into the weapon at one time for rapid reloading and firing.

The security check performed for the attorney did little to keep Biro from breaking into the office, which he accomplished by slipping through the transom. It also did nothing to prevent him from making off with the deadly weapon, in a handy carrying case, that was left unlocked in a desk drawer.

The story of the unsecured handgun that Biro so easily stole raises, once again, the foolhardy intransigence of the NRA's opposition to mandatory safe-storage laws, which it equates with unreasonable restrictions on the right to own firearms. So Biro's attorney, by leaving a deadly rapid-fire handgun unlocked and easily accessible, violated no law when it was used in a murder. And now, with the gun industry immunity law in place, neither the maker nor the seller of a gun that is similarly left unlocked can be held liable in a civil action suit when it is used by someone like Biro. A court did, however, eventually hold the attorney from whom Biro stole the gun liable in a civil suit brought by Jennifer and her family.

With the .357 Magnum in his possession, Biro no longer needed the FOID card he had planned to steal back from the family's attorney. He was now equipped to achieve his avowed goal: finding out what it would be like to kill someone.

Jennifer remains convinced that Biro chose his victims randomly, and that he neither knew nor targeted them for killing. But he reportedly later told a friend that the young couple was just "so preppy American that they deserved to die," although he never has actually admitted to the murders to police or in court.

Said Jennifer, "It was like the targeting of the kids at Columbine. He picked 'Susy Cheerleader' and 'Joe Jock,' and that's who they were. Richard was an amazing athlete, and Nancy was a professional actress in Chicago. They drove Saabs, the whole thing." She is certain their killer had contempt for everything they stood for.

Biro, according to a friend to whom he reportedly confessed the details of his crime, gained entry to the home by using the glass cutters he had, along with other burglary tools. He sat in a reclining chair in the family room and waited for the couple to return home from the birthday dinner they had attended. When they were confronted by the waiting intruder, the couple's first thought was that they were being robbed. Nancy had just cashed her paycheck that day and immediately reached into her purse for $500 and reportedly asked him to take it, the stereo, the TV—anything he wanted, thinking he would be satisfied and leave.

But Jennifer said Biro simply threw the cash on the floor, saying it was not what he wanted. It was at that point that Nancy apparently told him she was pregnant and pleaded with him to not hurt her unborn baby.

There seemed to be some hope for survival at that point, because Biro allegedly told the couple that he wasn't going to hurt them and would only lock them in the basement while he made his getaway. He forced them to walk down the stairs to the basement, keeping the Magnum trained on them. When they reached the bottom, without warning he aimed the gun point-blank at the back of Richard's head and fired, "just blowing his brains out, killing him instantly," according to Jennifer.

Nancy began pleading with the gunman not to harm her baby. She clasped her hands across her abdomen, sobbing. And without saying a word, Biro lowered the gun to take aim directly at her belly and fired, killing both mother and unborn child.

Jennifer recounted how the force of the bullet

had destroyed the fetus to the point that, in an autopsy, it was impossible to determine the gender of the unborn child, denying the family even the ability to give it a name for the funeral.

"The absolute worst part of my sister's death," said Jennifer, "was that she apparently lay on the floor in agony for thirty minutes before dying. We saw evidence of her attempts to pull herself across the basement floor, losing blood. She eventually managed to drag herself across the room to her husband's body and, with her own blood, she drew a heart and a 'U' next to his head—leaving her final message for him, 'Love you,' and then died.

"For me, my journey begins with that message," said Jennifer, her voice breaking. "I could not think about those last thirty minutes of her life for a long time. It was just too much for me. I did deal with things like the press, the long murder investigation … it was all a nightmare. The kid didn't get caught for six months. It was a huge story in Chicago for the entire time, a story that just would not go away."

Eventually, Biro began to talk about what he had kept secret for months. He confided in students at school, saying such startling things as, "You know those two murders that happened in town? Well, I did them."

Of course, no one took him seriously. Here was a sixteen-year-old student matter-of-factly boasting of the most shocking double murder in memory in that affluent, seemingly safe suburban community.

Biro would talk in detail about the murders to anyone who would listen, and then would eventually say, "Oh, I'm just kidding you."

Jennifer said, "But then he tells one friend, a newly arrived immigrant student from Vietnam who had trouble understanding English, the whole story, with every detail of the murders. And that young man sat on the information for months, not knowing if he could believe Biro. But ultimately Biro told the student that he was going to do it again, in a bank this time, where he would shoot all the tellers, take millions of dollars, and go to Mexico. It was at that point that the young man from Vietnam went to local police and essentially said, 'You know, you should investigate this guy Biro.' So the police executed a search warrant for Biro's bedroom, and what did they find, after six months of dead-end investigations? A .357 Magnum with a perfect ballistic match to the bullets that killed my sister and brother-in-law. They found the glass cutters, the handcuffs—everything, even a glove that matched one that was left at the murder scene."

Biro was immediately arrested, and Jennifer and her shocked family were notified of the break in the case. Justice then moved quickly, as prosecutors even attempted to get the Illinois legislature to memorialize the victims with a juvenile death penalty bill that would allow execution of a sixteen-year-old murderer.

"It was horrible, talk of the death penalty. All I could think about was how did this kid get a gun, and why was it he would want to do this? And what did the state mean, that they wanted to kill even more children with the death penalty as a way of responding to this?"

Biro was tried and convicted in just two weeks. He never confessed. His defense included an accusation that someone else, a friend, committed the murders. Tried as an adult, Biro was convicted of three counts of first-degree murder, one of the counts for the killing of the unborn fetus in its mother's womb. The jury took only two hours to reach the verdicts, which carried three consecutive life prison sentences with no chance for parole.

To add a final, tragic note to the horrific story, Jennifer revealed that Biro, now thirty years old, is incarcerated in a maximum-security state prison, a very old prison, almost medieval, in Jennifer's words. When asked if she had visited the prison and if so, why, she replied, "I got to see it as part of my work on behalf of ending the death penalty."

Ordinary people thrust into extraordinary circumstance appropriately describes what happened to Jennifer Bishop and her family. In thirty horrible minutes, pure chance plunged a happy, functional family into a dark pit of despair that few people can imagine.

Survivors like Jennifer tell their stories, as painful as they are to recount, in the hope that they can turn their personal loss into a passionate pursuit of an end to the gun violence epidemic.

In a twist of irony, Jennifer's personal encounter

with gun violence led to her meeting the man she would marry, Bill Jenkins, who, like her, lost a loved one, a young son who was shot to death in 1997 in the robbery of the restaurant where he worked.

Jennifer and Bill, both divorced at the time, first met at a national conference on victim advocacy in 2001. Jennifer knew of Bill Jenkins, a college professor, and of the popular book he had authored, *What to Do When the Police Leave: A Guide to the First Days of Traumatic Loss.* More than 20,000 copies have been sold, and the book continues to provide insights and guidance to surviving loved ones of murder victims.

One year after they met, the two were married, and they both continue to work in behalf of murder victim assistance and ending gun violence.

Bill Jenkins spoke freely of the tragedy that changed his life forever, in the same way Jennifer's changed hers.

"My son, William, was just sixteen. It was his second day of work in his new job at a fast-food restaurant in Richmond, Virginia. A twenty-three-year-old man armed with a semiautomatic handgun accosted William as the restaurant was closing and forced him at gunpoint to take him inside. When the manager, a young woman, opened the door to let them in, the robber suddenly shot William in the back for unknown reasons. After forcing the woman to open the restaurant safe, the robber fled with $1,700 in cash and the woman's purse."

Two accomplices, both females, aged seventeen

and eighteen, waited outside for the robber. It took only five minutes for local police to find and apprehend the trio, who had not even tried to leave the area but remained across the street from the scene of the crime. According to Bill, the murder weapon was obtained illegally by the seventeen-year-old.

Bill, like Jennifer, in spite of the rage within him over the killing of his son, did not want the death penalty, even though the prosecutor did. Six months after the murder, a jury convicted the killer of first-degree murder and sentenced him to life in prison with no possibility of parole. Again, like the killer of Jennifer's sister and brother-in-law, the gunman will spend the rest of his life behind prison bars.

"I'm at peace with my decision not to ask the court for the death penalty," said Bill. "I know I did the right thing when I read about another murder in which the killer was sentenced to death. I tracked down the family of the victim, who told me, 'We waited for eight years for the killer's execution. We could not move on all that time.'"

Bill seemed to echo Jennifer's sentiment on the issue of the death penalty, saying that causing another death does nothing to ease the pain of loss, nor does it prevent future deaths of children.

Agree or not with Bill Jenkins or with his wife, Jennifer, on the question of the death penalty, one would be hard pressed to argue with their conviction that taking the life of a killer does not bring back the life that was taken. For them, and for so many who agree with them, it is not a fair trade, a life taken for a life lost. A former prosecutor in Denver, Colorado, Craig Silverman, who is now a talk-show host and consultant for news media on criminal justice issues, once explained to me, "In cases of murder, people speak about obtaining justice, sometimes with the death penalty. But the fact is, there can be no true justice when

Agree or not with Bill Jenkins or with his wife, Jennifer, on the question of the death penalty, one would be hard pressed to argue with their conviction that taking the life of a killer does not bring back the life that was taken.

someone is murdered, even with conviction and even the imposition of the death penalty. When the verdict is read, the murdered person does not come back to life. There can, however, be retribution. After the murder of a loved one, the world stops spinning in a normal way. When society reacts with harsh punishment, it starts to restore balance, and the world begins to revolve closer to the way it once did."

In Bill and Jennifer Jenkins's case, they find it far more important to turn their grief into action that might prevent similar tragedies from happening to other families. Rather than bitterly demand their retribution, they focus on the root causes of senseless gun violence.

"I think there's a lot of hope," said Bill when asked if he sees any chance of stemming the gun violence. "The problem is still with the NRA. Their only concern is with profits of the gun industry." It has become a familiar refrain, that characterization of the NRA as putting profits over public safety, as refusing to acknowledge the need for stronger gun laws that can keep guns and criminals far and irrevocably apart from one another.

Something else Bill Jenkins said about the NRA offers an interesting insight into its use of the Second Amendment as an excuse for intransigence: he told me that on a wall of the NRA's headquarters building, there is a message that is supposed to be the text of the Second Amendment to the Constitution. "But they conveniently left off half of the amendment wording," said Bill, "the half about a well-regulated militia."

That convenient omission may well be the most telling handwriting on any wall, including the NRA's, in the ongoing argument over the true intent of that 200-year-old amendment.

———

As the NRA continues to successfully apply pressure to the nation's lawmakers with the constant threat of reprisal, there are voices in Congress who ignore the pressure and are willing to take the risk to their careers, standing up to do the right thing on the gun issue. One of the strongest of those voices is another victim of gun terror who turned tragedy into a life's mission to stop the violence, Representative Carolyn McCarthy of New York.

She represents a conservative area in suburban Long Island, a Democrat who continues to be reelected in a Republican-dominated district. To spend some time with the demure yet outspoken nurse-turned-widow-turned-congresswoman is to understand why she prevails over partisan politics.

I met with her in her office in the House of Representatives' Cannon Office Building on a day when the halls of Congress were buzzing with breaking news that would soon force Republican Majority Leader Tom DeLay to resign his post: his indictment on money-laundering and conspiracy charges.

The news prompted her to begin the conversation with an assessment of her party's chances to make gains in the Republican-controlled House and, as a result, get that body moving forward again on gun issues. Speaking of the storm clouds gathering over the opposition party, she held her hands in front of her, palms facing upward, as though holding something large, and said, "God just handed us something on a big silver platter. If we drop it, we have no one to blame but ourselves."

Does that make her, above all, a partisan, out to seize any advantage over the party she feels stands in the way of progress in her war against gun violence? She would be the first to admit, unapologetically, that it does. For when she was first elected to Congress in 1996, never having run for political office before, she made it clear that she was on a mission to do something about the gun violence that took the life of her husband and nearly killed her son as well.

The event that changed Carolyn McCarthy's life forever happened three years before her first run for Congress, on December 7, 1993. A headline of a column, written by Paul Vitello in *Newsday*, a Long Island newspaper, reads "Gunfire on the 5:33. Colin Ferguson opens fire on a rush-hour LIRR train, killing six in a shocking spree."

The column recalled the otherwise routine departure of the late-afternoon train from Manhattan, carrying commuters who worked in New York City home to suburban Long Island. Half an hour later, the train pulled into Garden City with twenty-five victims of Colin Ferguson's rampage, shot at point-blank range in what the perpetrator later described as revenge for an imagined government conspiracy against him. Of those twenty-five victims, six died of their wounds and the remaining nineteen were seriously wounded.

One of the dead was Denis McCarthy, Carolyn's husband. And one of the more seriously wounded was their son, Kevin, who suffered a life-threatening head wound and underwent a painfully slow recovery described as miraculous.

That deadly journey of the 5:33 began Carolyn McCarthy's own journey, which led her to Washington, D.C., where she continues a fight she vows will never end until America comes to its senses and confronts the forces that allowed her personal tragedy to happen.

The meeting with the congresswoman in the fall of 2005 was my second encounter with her. The first was six years earlier, in 1999, shortly after the Columbine massacre, when I helped lead a trip to Washington with ninety-nine students, which included a meeting with President Bill Clinton and an opportunity to lobby members of Congress for stronger gun regulation. The congresswoman apparently heard that our group was gathered outside the Capitol, and she dropped what she was doing, searching us out to personally welcome us to Washington and to thank the students for their efforts. She was an inspiration to the young people, most of whom had never been to the nation's capital, let alone met a president or members of Congress.

When asked what specifically moved her to enter politics, the congresswoman replied, "What brought me to Washington was when my son, Kevin, was in rehab from his injuries in the shooting and was learning how to speak again. He wanted to know how this could have happened to him. And I didn't have that answer. At the same time, there were a few other surviving relatives of victims who started looking at the same question. There was also a campaign going on in New York with Governor Cuomo, who was trying to pass an assault weapons ban. Some of the victims became involved in that effort, and they approached me, asking me if I would go to Albany to lobby our assemblypeople for the ban."

She explained the change she had to undergo

when she became involved politically. "I was extremely quiet back then. I was very shy. My husband was outgoing, but I never liked being in crowds."

Her son urged her, in spite of her hesitancy to become a public persona, to get involved in the issue. She agreed to go to Albany with the other victims and try her hand at lobbying.

"I remember this long table and a bunch of state senators who had absolutely no interest in the issue, who could care less that there was a group of victims there talking to them. It's funny, then I didn't know what was going on. But now, sitting here in Washington, I know exactly what they were doing. They spent five minutes, as though they were interested, then posed for a picture for the press and planned on doing nothing. They told us they couldn't do the assault weapons ban because it was going to be attached to a death penalty bill. I didn't know at the time that it was what they call a 'poison pill.' It would just be killed with the other part of the bill that couldn't be separated out.

"So I said, okay, just give me scissors. I'll show you how to separate it out. Very simple."

It was the future congresswoman's first lesson in the realities of legislative politics. It was also the beginning of a continuing interest the New York media took in what she was trying to do with the state legislature.

"We always seemed to get a lot of press coverage. And it caught Governor Cuomo's eye. He was starting to fall in the polls. But being that he was trying to get the assault weapons ban passed, he asked me if I would do commercials for him. And I did."

It was somewhat of a problem for her. "I have dyslexia. I can't read a script. But I did a couple of commercials anyway. Then he asked me to speak for him at the Democratic Party's convention. I didn't really want to be a speaker, but he convinced me, and I just went there and talked about the gun issue, and asked why we need assault weapons. Now it wasn't just the train tragedy. You looked at the paper and saw how many people were being killed every day in New York, most of them children.

"Apparently I had a knack for speaking, in my own way, not polished. I'm still not. I get frustrated with myself, even to this day, when I hear my colleagues in the House speak and then I get up to speak. I'm very blunt. I don't say thank you to everybody. I just go right to the subject. It's probably my nursing background. You sit there and it's very frustrating. You have a room full of politicians who just keep tripping over each other saying thank you."

Her lobbying efforts in New York were soon noticed by national political figures, including President Bill Clinton, who was trying to get a national assault weapons ban passed. As a result of the press coverage she was getting in New York, she was contacted by Sarah and Jim Brady and asked to go to Washington to lobby members of Congress on the ban. Then the president and First Lady Hillary

Clinton asked her to get involved as well.

"That was how I became involved at the national level, in 1994. We got the assault weapons bill passed. I was present for the signing with the president. Then, when that was over and done with, here we were, these victims who had worked to get a bill passed, and we asked ourselves, 'Well, what do we do now?'"

In May 1995, Carolyn McCarthy answered the question, driven by anger over attempts by her congressman, Republican Dan Frisa, to kill the very bill she had worked so hard to see passed: the assault weapons ban that she believed could help prevent future tragedies like the Long Island Railroad massacre. A bill was introduced in the House to repeal the ban that had been passed the previous year. Carolyn appealed to Frisa to support keeping the ban in place, but he refused, choosing instead to vote for its repeal on the grounds that the original ban was flawed. Supporters of the ban prevailed, and it remained in place.

But for the feisty nurse from Mineola, her congressman's effort to reverse what she and her colleagues had worked so hard for was not something she could ignore. Her decision to make the first move into politics came on the steps of the Capitol after the vote on the weapons ban. A reporter for the *New York Daily News* approached her and asked, "Mrs. McCarthy, how mad are you?"

"I said, 'I'm really mad.' He said, 'Are you mad enough to run against Dan Frisa?' And I answered,

'Yes, I really am,' without even thinking anything about it."

The next morning, she went to visit Congressman Chuck Schumer and he greeted her with congratulations on her decision.

"What are you talking about?" she asked.

"You're running for Congress," he answered, beaming.

With exactly that much thought and preparation, Carolyn McCarthy was now suddenly a candidate for the United States Congress. The story hit the national wire services, and when she returned home, she was inundated with phone calls from people pledging support. Neighbors knocked on her door and offered to help. And the campaign began, but only after Carolyn, a registered Republican, was rebuffed by her party when she announced that she would oppose Frisa in a primary. She was then approached by the local Democratic Party, which pledged to support her if she would run on its ticket. During her deliberations over whether to take the Democrats up on their offer and make the run with them, Carolyn's son, Kevin, still in rehabilitation from his brain injury, made her a promise: "If you run and win," he said, "I promise I'll be able to dress myself by election day." And she did run. And he did dress himself.

On the first Tuesday following the first Monday of November 1996, she was elected with an impressive margin to the House of Representatives, where she was serving her fifth term at the time of this writing. She quickly became one of the leading congressional voices in the fight against the gun violence epidemic. In spite of no background in politics and no knowledge of how the game is played in the hallowed halls of government, she did what came naturally for her: she put her head down and went full speed ahead, driven by an innate sense of what was right and what was not. Her style is all about cutting through to the heart of the matter, like picking up scissors to show how to separate one bill from another rather than getting bogged down in rhetoric. It worked well for her. Before long she was being praised by national magazines and political pundits as a leading Washington advocate for sensible gun laws, and she remains in the forefront of that issue, never yielding to pressures of the gun lobby, which has been unable to drive her out of office, much as they might wish to.

She was also lauded for not being a single-issue congresswoman, focusing not only on the gun issue but on other things that truly mattered to her constituents back home in Long Island, specifically health care, seniors issues, and the financial impact of government policies on working people of her district.

As I interviewed Carolyn McCarthy and witnessed her passion for doing the right thing, I could not help but think of another Congresswoman—Pat Schroeder—who, nearly three decades earlier, took on the establishment in her own party and, later, in the House of Representatives. Representative Schroeder went to Washington from Colorado in 1972, and served for twelve distinguished terms. Like Carolyn McCarthy, Pat Schroeder was politically unknown in her district. She ran as a breath of fresh air, against the advice of the "experts" who gave her no chance of even winning the Democratic primary against a man, let alone the general election and a seat in the House. She based her effort on a sense of what was wrong in the country at the time, namely the war in Vietnam. She also opposed the staging of the winter Olympics in her home state after the games had already been awarded to Denver. She defied the odds. She ran against the grain and never once took a poll. She simply followed her heart and her instincts, and she won the seat, beginning a career in which she quickly became a force with which to contend, to the consternation of the "good old boys club" that she challenged and poked. She won a seat on the powerful House Armed Services Committee, which was unheard of for a woman. The war she had spoken out against was soon opposed by a majority of Americans, which led to the end of the career of President Lyndon Johnson. The winter Olympics she opposed were cancelled in Colorado by a vote of the people. And Pat Schroeder was again proved right. She even approached the biggest political stage of all, presidential politics, but declined to mount it, to the disappointment of a large and dedicated national constituency she developed in Congress.

Both Pat Schroeder and Carolyn McCarthy

proved that the process of politics and the people who practice it, in spite of the declining esteem in which politicians are held today, can still shape a better world. Pat opposed a war her conscience told her was wrong. Carolyn waged a war that her conscience dictated was right.

It's enough to renew one's faith in one's vote.

———

As a student at Columbine High School, Daniel Mauser's passion was debate. Issues of the day were important to him. In April 1999, he read an article in *Time* about gun laws in America. He was troubled by something he learned in the article and asked his father over dinner, "Did you know there are dangerous loopholes in the gun laws in this country?"

Two weeks later, on April 20, Daniel lay dead in his high school, along with thirteen other students and one teacher. Two of the students who died that day were the heavily armed perpetrators of the worst school massacre in history, which came to be known around the world simply as "Columbine." Daniel's earlier concern about the dangers of weak gun laws took on a tragic prescience when it was discovered that three of the four weapons used in the murder of his classmates, himself, a teacher trying to protect them, and, finally, in the suicide of the two shooters, passed through what has come to be known as the "gun show loophole," a loophole that his father would play a critical role in closing in Colorado a year and a half later.

The Mauser family—Tom, his wife, Linda, and their two children, Daniel, fifteen, and Christie, twelve—was leading what would can best be described as an ordinary life. They were close-knit, church-going people, enjoying the quality of life in a suburban Denver community. Then, like the thousands of other victims of gun violence, the ordinary life the Mauser family was living was thrust into the extraordinary on that day of insanity at Columbine.

"The worst part of that day," said Tom Mauser, "was that awful wait. We were summoned to a nearby elementary school where, we were told, students who had survived the attack would be reunited with their parents."

But as the hours dragged on painfully, Tom and Linda realized their son would not be coming back with the others on the school buses that pulled up and discharged the terrified young students into the waiting arms of their tearful parents. It was not until the following morning that police officially informed Tom and Linda what they had already known, that Daniel had been fatally shot.

Tom made it clear in the interview that he preferred not to go over, yet again, a painful recounting of the awful day. He explained that he knows no more details of the massacre than what the rest of the world learned in their newspapers and on the pervasive television coverage that ensued in the days and months following the killings.

"Even if I tried to go over the details of what happened, I wouldn't be able to. Because to this day everything that happened is still just a blur," he said.

He added that he likely would have remained as reclusive as possible, resisting the many requests for interviews by national and international media. But something happened to change his wish to remain out of the spotlight: the annual convention of the National Rifle Association was scheduled to take place in Denver just twelve days after Columbine. The mayor of Denver at the time, Wellington Webb, had appealed to the NRA to postpone or cancel its May 1 meeting, out of respect for the grieving of not just the surviving families of Columbine but for the entire state that was mourning the tragedy.

The NRA agreed to shorten its meeting schedule but refused to call off the most incendiary event, a speech by firebrand Charlton Heston, famous for holding a rifle over his head and declaring defiantly, "from my cold, dead hands," the inciting rallying cry of gun owners who believe their rights are in danger of being pried from them.

On the day of Heston's speech, a hastily organized demonstration attended by thousands took place on the steps of the Colorado capitol to protest the NRA's appearance and what was viewed as insensitive timing. One of the protest's organizers, Ted Pascoe of Physicians for Social Responsibility, contacted Tom and asked him to appear and speak at the rally.

"I've never been a public speaker, and wasn't

inclined to start being one," said Tom. "It was so soon after Daniel's death. But, I was really angered that Charlton Heston would be railing against gun controls right here in Colorado."

It was at that rally, holding a handmade sign that said, "My son, Daniel Mauser, died at Columbine," that the soft-spoken and grieving father found the strength to speak and began his journey of activism in memory of his fallen son. Tom's heartfelt message was greeted by silent reverence as he explained the personal impact of the tragedy on him and his family.

"I am Tom Mauser, father of Daniel Mauser. … For my family, these past days have represented a flash flood. That is, we witnessed a momentary, senseless, horrific flash of hatred and violence. It has been followed by an amazing flood of tears, prayers, calls, cards, visits, and countless expressions of sympathy and love. Now the question is whether the floodwaters can be channeled into something meaningful or whether they'll be followed by another flash flood in another unsuspecting community."

Turning to his anger at the NRA's intransigence on the issue, he continued, "For years the NRA has told us that if we just locked up our criminals, we'd be safe. Well, we've built thousands more jail cells and locked people up, but the killing goes on. My son was not killed by criminals—they only became criminals once they pulled the triggers. The NRA's prison cells haven't solved the problem. In fact, it seems it's now *us* who are locked up—in fear!"

It was a transformation that day of an ordinary, quiet man who had been sufficiently angered at the injustice done to his son and family into someone who now had to speak out, to act. The first act, after addressing the protestors, was to join them as they marched peacefully the two blocks to where Heston was speaking and encircle the building, some holding signs calling for an end to the violence of guns, others singing the civil rights hymn "We Shall Overcome." Mayor Webb, who first won election in his famous walk of the city, in which he took to the streets of Denver when his campaign could not afford an expensive television effort, was back walking again. This time it was with the group of grieving, angry Coloradans who made it clear to Heston that his inflammatory rhetoric was not welcome in the Columbine state.

> "For years the NRA has told us that if we just locked up our criminals, we'd be safe. Well, we've built thousands more jail cells and locked people up, but the killing goes on. My son was not killed by criminals—they only became criminals once they pulled the triggers."
>
> —Tom Mauser,
> board president of
> Colorado Ceasefire

It was also on that Saturday that an idea was born: to band together and do something about the loophole in the gun laws that had troubled Daniel Mauser just two weeks before it figured in his death. It was agreed by several of us who attended the protest to form a grassroots movement that was to be called SAFE Colorado (Sane Alternative to the Firearms Epidemic) and to answer the question, "What can we do against the powerful gun lobby to stop the violence?"

Tom Mauser went on to play a key role in the activities of the new organization. And he has never stopped his activism nor, he says confidently, will he in the future. He was invited to the White House by First Lady Hillary Clinton to address a group advocating for violence reduction. He began traveling the country to speak on the subject of needed gun regulation, always opening his remarks by bending down and removing a pair of running shoes he wore. He would hold them above his head, not unlike the way Charlton Heston would hold a gun, and say, "These are the shoes my son, Daniel, was wearing when he was shot at Columbine. I am walking in them today. And I will continue walking in them, for Daniel."

> "These are the shoes my son, Daniel, was wearing when he was shot at Columbine. I am walking in them today. And I will continue walking in them, for Daniel."
>
> —Tom Mauser, board president of Colorado Ceasefire

Something else that Tom and Linda felt should be done to help the family move on was to bring another child into the family. They turned to China, where they knew they would find a child in need of a home, and they adopted a one-year-old girl, Madeline, at great financial sacrifice. Five years later, when I went to the Mauser home to interview Tom, there was an outgoing and strikingly pretty little girl, so polite, so full of enthusiasm for the approaching Christmas holiday, eager to show the decorations and the gingerbread houses she had made with her parents. It felt like everyone's notion of a happy home at a happy time. Still, it is hard not to wonder how much of a hole remains in that close-knit family.

When Tom and Linda first adopted Madeline, a reporter wrote that it was an attempt to replace Daniel. I asked Tom about the comment. His response was "No, it was a tribute to Daniel, not a replacement. People are irreplaceable."

Tom celebrates Daniel's life with a Web site that has been up and running since shortly after his death. He always encourages everyone he meets to visit the site to learn more about the son he lost and about the unending efforts by groups he works with to stop the violence that grips the country. The site's address is www.DanielMauser.com.

One story that can be found on the site tells how Tom, who had never been charged in his entire life with breaking even the most minor of laws, has now been arrested twice. In both cases, it was on charges of trespassing when he protested the NRA's opposition to all gun reforms at the organization's national headquarters in Virginia. For walking on the sidewalk, which was NRA property, to deliver his message, he was arrested and fined based on the NRA's complaint, proving that the behemoth lobby is threatened by a single man who silently protests in his late son's memory. But he remains undeterred, and, if need be, he will face arrest again to make his point, for Daniel and for the nearly 30,000 other gun victims who will likely die this year.

I asked Tom the same question I asked Sarah Brady: "Why is the United States the most gun violent of all industrialized nations, with more deaths from firearms than all the other countries combined?"

His answer was different from Sarah's, who had said, "We haven't grown up yet." He replied, "We don't trust our own government."

He explained that there is a widely held notion among the more rigid opponents of gun legislation that the government is somehow an adversary that is waiting for the opportunity to seize every citizen's guns, along with every freedom.

"It's so absurd," he said. "If we can't trust our own government, we're saying we can't trust ourselves, because who is the government? It's us."

Finally, I asked Tom what his wish list is for reversing gun violence, what steps he feels need to be taken to prevent future Columbines from happening. His response:

- **There must be registration of all guns,** a notion that is so fiercely feared and fought by the gun lobby. It matters not that we accept registration of the cars we drive, the boats we use, the airplanes we fly in. Guns, somehow, must be excluded from the traceability and accountability implicit in registration. Register our guns, and they will soon be taken from us, says the gun lobby, instilling bogus fears in the hearts of even moderate gun owners and hunters. When an opponent of registration is asked why, if their fears of seizure are valid, have there not been wholesale seizure of Americans' cars, boats, and planes, the answer, generally, is something to the effect that the Constitution does not grant the right to drive a car, but it does ensure the right to own a gun—at best, a self-serving non sequitur.

- **Existing gun laws must be taken more seriously.** Tom points out that loopholes continue to exist in laws regulating firearm sales, especially at gun shows and in private sales, loopholes like the one through which three Columbine murder weapons passed. His state, Colorado, was the first of two states in the nation to enact a law to close the gun show loophole, but all efforts to enact a national loophole-closing law in all states have been defeated, thanks again to the powerful gun lobby.

- **The assault weapons ban must be reinstated.** The Bush administration and the Republican majority in both houses of Congress allowed the ban to expire in 2005, giving the gun industry yet another victory. Tom offered the reminder that Daniel was killed at Columbine with a carbine equipped with a fifteen-shot clip, making it an assault weapon that would be banned if the law were reinstated.
- **Safe storage of guns must be mandated by law.** So many of the thousands of accidental gun deaths are the result of someone finding or stealing a gun that is carelessly left, often loaded, within easy reach of a child or a criminal. A gun under a mattress or on a closet shelf is not safely stored if someone can easily find it and use it. Uniform safe-storage laws would punish gun owners whose negligence, through unsafe storage, causes death or bodily harm.

Tom's wish list is hardly the work of a radical, of a "gun-grabber," as those who oppose such measures would call him. Rather, those measures are what the majority of Americans find perfectly acceptable. What prevents them from becoming laws of the land is the minority of Americans who have such a powerful hold on the political process.

In Conclusion, and in Hope

Why did I choose to write this book? Because I cling to the hope that we, as a nation, will come to our senses and take whatever steps are necessary to put an end to the gun violence that continues to exact its enormous toll.

We are a country of decent people, yet we allow indecent things to happen to innocent victims, often defenseless children. What else is it, if not indecency, when we are the most heavily armed of all developed nations with the highest incident of gun deaths as well, which is hardly a coincidence.

> We are a country of decent people, yet we allow indecent things to happen to innocent victims, often defenseless children.

There are those who continue to stand in the way of reasonable controls of guns, claiming virtually everyone is entitled to buy and use firearms, even automatic weapons of destruction, claiming that more guns means less crime. The arguments are as specious as they are transparent efforts to give special treatment to a single industry. It is the industry that makes and markets the weapons that killed the children at Columbine, the countless victims of violent crime, the battered wives, the scores of police officers doing their sworn duty.

From the beginning, guns were designed for a single purpose: to kill. The Second Amendment to the U.S. Constitution was written to ensure that militias, the first defense against the young nation's enemies, were sufficiently armed. The NRA and the radical elements of the gun rights movement continue to argue that the amendment was intended to grant all individuals, not only well-regulated militias, the absolute right to gun ownership and use. I am confident they will one day be judged wrong.

It seems likely that the judiciary will eventually rule on the question of the Second Amendment's intent and meaning, to the dismay of the gun lobby. In fact, it is generally believed in more-moderate circles that the last thing the gun industry wants to see is a Supreme Court ruling on the intent of the amendment to which they so tenaciously cling. They surely must see the handwriting on the wall that one day will say, Gun ownership is not an absolute right given to all persons, particularly when some of those persons turn out to be criminals, the mentally unstable, and, now, in the twenty-first century, terrorists bent on our destruction.

The issue of access to guns is, of course, a divisive one, one which many believe provides no hope for accommodation or resolution. But, for the sake of public safety and law and order, let us hope they are wrong. I, for one, firmly believe there *is* common ground on which we can resolve the issues that divide the states and the nation. The successful effort to close the gun show loophole in Colorado was testament to our ability to find that common ground. Success came through bringing people together rather than driving them apart. Hunters joined with educators and clergy to call for an end to the violence; Republicans stood with Democrats; elderly joined hands with young people, as did men with women of conscience. It was a large tent under which the effort flourished and succeeded.

Sarah Brady said in this book that the reason this nation is so prone to gun violence is simply that we have not yet grown up. She may be right. And if she is, there are ways to guide us toward a new maturity of thought on the issue.

With the tireless efforts of survivors of gun tragedies, with the courageous refusal of some political leaders to be intimidated by powerful lobbies, and with the commitment of countless thousands of everyday citizens, perhaps just like you, dear reader, we can finally achieve what was once thought impossible: not a disarming of America, but a rearming of our will to do the right thing.

Let us hope that we will soon achieve that urgent goal. For the children in our schools. For the police who protect us. For the random victims of gun terror. For the deeply troubled who resort to taking their own lives. For America, the Beautiful. For America, the Safe.

Appendix
How Safe Are You?

Just how safe from gun violence you and your family are could well depend on where you live. The Brady Campaign has created a safety scoring system that assigns a letter grade, from A to F, to all states. The grading is based on the presence or absence of laws that fall into seven categories of gun regulations that are intended to shield families from gun violence:

- Juvenile possession laws
- Juvenile sale/transfer laws
- Gun safety locks and safer design standards
- Child access prevention
- Laws that allow cities to regulate guns (non-preemption laws)
- Secondary "private" sales background checks
- Carrying concealed weapons laws (which strictly limit or ban carrying in public)

Violence prevention advocates point to a correlation between meaningful firearms regulation and lower gun-violence incidence. That correlation is borne out by a recent state-by-state compilation of firearm death rates in the United States. The state with the highest ranking in the country, and the lowest death rate, is Hawaii; it is also a state assigned an A- grade for having gun laws on the books in all seven categories.

Conversely, the state with the poorest ranking, fiftieth, and the highest death rate, Louisiana, has earned a grade of F, with virtually no regulations in the seven categories, except one law that requires juveniles to be seventeen to possess a handgun.

Perhaps the most telling conclusion that can be drawn from the data is a refutation of the rallying cry of gun law opponents: that more laws do not mean less violence. Clearly, from this data, they do.

State	Grade	Deaths per 100,000	National Ranking	Juvenile Possession Law	Juvenile Sales/Transfer Law	Child Access Prevention	Gun Safety Lock Standards	Non-Preemption	Secondary Private Sales Background Checks	Carrying Concealed Weapons Limits
Alabama	F	17.39	46	No	Yes	No	No	No	No	Some
Alaska	F+	18.50	49	Yes	No	No	No	No	No	No
Arizona	D	15.21	42	Yes	Yes	No	No	No	No	Some
Arkansas	D	15.15	41	Yes	Yes	No	No	No	No	Some*
California	A-	9.77	19	Yes	Yes	Yes	Yes	Yes	Yes	Yes
Colorado	D	11.01	26	Yes	Yes	No	No	No	Some*	Some
Connecticut	A	4.39	4	Yes	Yes	Yes	Yes	Yes	Yes	Yes
Delaware	C	7.95	13	Yes	Yes	Yes	No	Yes*	No	Yes
Florida	F+	11.40	30	Yes	Yes	Yes	No	Some	Yes*	No
Georgia	D	13.51	36	Yes	Yes	No	No	No	No	No
Hawaii	A-	2.94	1	Yes	Yes	Yes	Yes	Yes	Yes	Yes
Idaho	F+	12.00	33	Yes	Yes	No	No	No	No	No
Illinois	A-	9.06	16	Yes	Yes	Yes*	Yes	Yes	Yes	Yes
Indiana	D	11.23	29	Yes	Yes	Yes*	No	Yes*	No	No
Iowa	C+	7.07	10	Yes	Yes	Yes	No	No	Yes	Yes
Kansas	C-	11.16	28	Yes	Yes	Yes*	No	No	No	Yes
Kentucky	F	13.60	37	Yes	Yes	No	No	No	No	No
Louisiana	F	18.84	50	Yes*	Yes	No	No	No	No	No
Maine*	D-	6.28	7	No	Yes	Yes*	Yes*	No	No	No

State	Grade	Deaths per 100,000	National Ranking	Juvenile Posession Law	Juvenile Sales/Transfer Law	Child Access Prevention	Gun Safety Lock Standards	Non-Preemption	Secondary Private Sales Background Checks	Carrying Concealed Weapons Limits
Maryland	A-	11.76	32	Yes	Yes	Yes	Yes	Yes*	Yes	Yes
Massachusetts	A-	3.17	2	Yes	Yes	Yes	Yes	Yes	Yes	Yes
Michigan	D+	10.22	23	Yes	Yes	No	Some	No	Yes	No*
Minnesota	C-	6.56	8	Yes	Yes	Yes	Some	Yes*	No	No*
Mississippi	F	16.56	44	Yes	Yes	No	No	No	No	No
Missouri	D+	11.52	31	Yes	Yes	No	No	No	Yes	No*
Montana	F	15.80	43	Yes*	No	Yes*	No	Yes*	No	No*
Nebraska	B-	7.70	11	Yes	Yes	No	No	Some	Yes	Yes*
Nevada	D	16.69	45	Yes*	Yes	Yes	No	Yes	No	No
New Hampshire	D-	6.91	9	No	Yes	Yes	No	No	No	No
New Jersey	A-	5.30	5	Yes	Yes	Yes	Yes	Yes	Yes	Yes
New Mexico	F	17.39	47	Yes	No	No	No	No	No	No
New York	B+	5.39	6	Yes	Yes	No	Some	Yes	Yes	Yes
North Carolina	C	12.55	34	Yes	Yes	Yes	No	No	Yes	Yes*
North Dakota	D	9.15	17	Yes	Yes	No	No	No	No	No*
Ohio	D-	8.17	14	No	Yes	No	No	Yes	No	No*
Oklahoma	D-	12.79	35	Yes	Yes	No	No	No	No	No*
Oregon	C-	11.10	27	Yes	Yes	No	No	Yes*	Some*	No*
Pennsylvania	D+	9.95	22	Yes	Yes	No	Some	No	Yes	No

State	Grade	Deaths per 100,000	National Ranking	Juvenile Posession Law	Juvenile Sales/Transfer Law	Child Access Prevention	Gun Safety Lock Standards	Non-Preemption	Secondary Private Sales Background Checks	Carrying Concealed Weapons Limits
Rhode Island	B-	3.25	3	Yes	Yes	Yes	Some	No	Yes	Yes
South Carolina	D+	14.30	38	Yes	Yes	No	Some	No	No	No*
South Dakota	D	9.94	21	Yes	Yes	No	No	No	No	No
Tennessee	D+	14.33	39	Yes	Yes	No	No	No	No	No
Texas	D-	11.00	25	No	Yes	Yes	No	No	No	No*
Utah	D-	9.77	20	Yes	Yes	No	No	No	No	No
Vermont	D-	7.75	12	Yes	Yes	No	No	No	No	No
Virginia	C-	10.98	24	Yes	Yes	Yes	No	No	No	No
Washington	D+	9.21	18	Yes	Yes	No	No	Yes*	No	No
West Virginia	D	14.64	40	Yes	Yes	No	No	No	No	No*
Wisconsin	C+	8.55	15	Yes	Yes	Yes	No	No	No	Yes
Wyoming	F	17.75	48	No	No	No	No	No	No	No

Arkansas: **Carrying Concealed Weapons Limits**—allowed in parks and restaurants
Colorado: **Secondary Private Sales Background Checks**—at gun shows
Delaware: **Non-Preemption**—very restricted
Florida: **Secondary Private Sales Background Checks**—limited
Illinois: **Child Access Prevention**—weak penalties
Indiana: **Child Access Prevention**—weak penalties; **Non-Preemption**—minimal
Kansas: **Child Access Prevention**—partial
Lousiana: **Juvenile Posession Law**—only on handguns

Maine: Even with a poor grade for gun laws, enjoys a low per capita gun rate and a high ranking as a result; **Child Access Prevention**—partial; **Gun Safety Lock Standards**—minimal

Maryland: **Non-Preemption**—minimal

Michigan: **Carrying Concealed Weapons Limits**—training required

Minnesota: **Non-Preemption**—minimal; **Carrying Concealed Weapons Limits**—training required

Missouri: **Carrying Concealed Weapons Limits**—no police discretion to deny a permit, training, no legal reciprocity between states

Montana: **Juvenile Posession Law**—partial; **Child Access Prevention**—partial; **Non-Preemption**—parks only; **Carrying Concealed Weapons Limits**—training required

Nebraska: **Carrying Concealed Weapons Limits**—prohibited

Nevada: **Juvenile Posession Law**—with broad exemptions for children over 14

North Carolina: **Carrying Concealed Weapons Limits**—no police discretion or required training

North Dakota: **Carrying Concealed Weapons Limits**—training required with strong limits

Ohio: **Carrying Concealed Weapons Limits**—strong limits

Oklahoma: **Carrying Concealed Weapons Limits**—training required

Oregon: **Non-Preemption**—limited; **Secondary Private Sales Background Checks**—at gun shows; **Carrying Concealed Weapons Limits**—banned in schools only

South Carolina: **Carrying Concealed Weapons Limits**—limits guns in cars

Texas: **Carrying Concealed Weapons Limits**—strong background check

Washington: **Non-Preemption**—very limited

West Virginia: **Carrying Concealed Weapons Limits**—training required

Data in this chart was gathered from the Brady Campaign to Prevent Gun Violence Web site, www.stategunlaws.org.

Discussion Questions

In the book, it is noted that a gun in a home is twenty-two times more likely to kill a resident of that home than an intruder. Given that statistic, do you feel a gun kept in a home for protection, particularly with children living there, is a wise, safe idea?

The National Rifle Association claims to speak for all gun owners. It claims a membership of 4 million people. Yet there are 70 million gun owners in America, which means only 5.7 percent of them are members of the NRA. What does this say about the NRA's claim that it represents all gun owners?

Do you know whether guns are kept in homes where your children go to play with their friends? Do you feel it is appropriate to ask if there are? If you keep any guns in your home, would you resent being asked about them by other parents?

In the book, Sarah Brady gives one reason why the United States is the most gun violent of all industrialized nations: because we haven't yet grown up. Tom Mauser, father of a murdered Columbine student, Daniel, offers another reason: because we don't trust our own government. Do you agree with either reason, or both, or neither? What reasons would you offer?

More and more cities and states are passing laws that allow permits for carrying concealed handguns in public to anyone who can pass a criminal background check. Do you agree with this trend? If so, why? If not, why not? Do you know what the law is in your community?

Should all firearms be registered and their sales records kept on file by law enforcement, just as for automobiles?

Is it fair to hold gun owners who do not safely store their weapons out of reach of children or intruders legally responsible if those weapons kill or injure in accidents or in crimes committed after their theft?

The assault weapons ban was allowed to die when Congress recently refused to extend it. Do you think this inaction places the populace at greater risk as a result?

What place do assault weapons and armor-piercing ammunition have in our society?

Congress recently passed a firearms industry immunity bill, which essentially prevents any lawsuits against manufacturers or distributors of deadly weapons that kill or injure people accidentally or in criminal acts by their owners. No other industry, including tobacco, asbestos, or alcohol, enjoys such immunity from liability. Is this equitable?